Praying through Life

How to pray in the home,
at work and in the family

Praying through Life

How to pray in the home, at work and in the family

STEPHEN COTTRELL

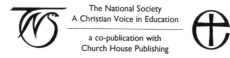

The National Society
A Christian Voice in Education

a co-publication with
Church House Publishing

National Society/Church House Publishing
Church House
Great Smith Street
London SW1P 3NZ

ISBN 0 7151 4902 4

Published 1998 by The National Society and Church House Publishing

Cover design by Leigh Hurlock

Printed in England by The Cromwell Press Ltd, Trowbridge, Wiltshire

With *prayer goes gratitude*

Julian of Norwich

For Joseph, Benjamin and Samuel
who have taught me to be thankful

Contents

Contents

Acknowledgements

I would like to thank Hamish Bruce at Church House Publishing for his encouragement to write this book; Jane Way, Celia McCulloch, Frances Bell, Pam Priestly, Marian Allmark, Dick Swindell and Pat Dixon in the Wakefield diocese all of whom worked with me producing material on prayer for our parishes; and my colleague Tim Sledge who looked over the text and made many helpful comments. Finally I wish to remember all those people I have prayed with on a regular basis and who have taught me so much, especially John Caldicott, Chris Newell, Daphne Bulwer, Maureen Jewell and Christina Inwood and to my wife Rebecca for her constant support and the companionship of her prayer.

Stephen Cottrell
Epiphany, 1998

Copyright acknowledgements

The publisher gratefully acknowledges permission to reproduce copyright material in this book. Every effort has been made to trace and contact copyright holders. If there are any inadvertent omissions we apologise to those concerned and will ensure that a suitable acknowledgement is made at the next reprint. Page numbers are indicated in parentheses.

Simon Bailey: From *Still with God*, National Society Enterprises/Church House Publishing, 1986, rev. edn 1993. Reproduced by permission of the publishers (**75,76**).

Bible Society: *Emmaus: The Way of Faith: Growing as a Christian*, copyright © Stephen Cottrell, Steve Croft, John Finney, Felicity Lawson and Robert Warren, published by National Society Enterprises Ltd/Church House Publishing and Bible Society 1996. Used with permission. (**10–2**).

Catholic Bishops' Conference of England and Wales: *A Pocket Ritual*, McCrimmon, 1977 (**47**).

The Central Board of Finance of the Church of England: *The Alternative Service Book* 1980 (**41**, **44**, **49**, **56**, **107–9**); *The Prayer Book as Proposed in* 1928 (**47**). Copyright © The Central Board of Finance of the Church of England and reproduced by permission.

Darton, Longman and Todd: Anon, *Rule for a New Brother*, 1973 (**11**, **122–23**); *New Jerusalem Bible*, published and copyright © 1985 Darton, Longman and Todd Ltd and Doubleday & Co Inc. Used by permission of the publishers.

Editions du Levain: Lucien Deiss, *Priéres bibliques*, 1974 (**49**, **55–6**).

The European Province of the Society of St Francis: *Celebrating Common Prayer*, 1992 (**56**, **108**).

Faber & Faber Ltd: W. H. Auden, Extract from *In Praise of Limestone*, in Collected Shorter Poems, 1966 (**130**).

Girl Guide Association: Prayer for world hunger (**52**).

Hodder & Stoughton Ltd: Frank Colquhoun, *Contemporary Parish Prayers*, 1975 (**47**, adapted); Richard Foster, *Prayer*, 1992 (**92**). Reproduced by permission of Hodder & Stoughton Ltd.

International Commission on English in the Liturgy: copyright © 1970, 1971, 1975 International Consultation on English Texts (ICET) (**42**).

Kingsway Publications: R. H. L. Williams, *More Prayers for Today's Church*, 1972, 1984.

HarperCollins Publishers Ltd: Michael Marshall, *Free to Worship*, Marshall Pickering, 1996 (**52–3**).

The National Society (Church of England) for Promoting Religious Education: Prayer by Mrs E. Rutter Leatham (**63**).

Michael Perry: From *Church Family Worship*, Hodder & Stoughton, 1986 (**72–3**, adapted).

Peterloo Poets: Extract from Friends' Meeting House, Frenchay, Bristol, No. 1 of 'Three Bristol Poems' from *Neck Verse*, copyright © U. A. Fanathorpe, 1992. Reproduced by permission (**95**).

SCM Press: Dietrich Bonhoeffer, *Letters and Papers from Prison*, enlarged edition, SCM Press, 1971 (**120**).

Introduction

Seeing the possibilities

Introduction
Seeing the possibilities

When we are invited to pray we are asked to open our tightly clenched fists and to give up our last coin.

Henri Nouwen, *Seeds of Hope*, pp.66–7.

I must begin with myself. Before I started writing this book I joked to a friend that I ought to sit at my desk wearing sackcloth and ashes. It seems such a terrible audacity to think that I have anything to say about prayer. God knows, and I know, just how half-hearted so much of my prayer has been, and how I have neglected prayer in so many areas of my life and on occasions too numerous to number.

You might think I am trying to put you off reading this book. It is just that you need to know from the outset that this is a book for novices. And it is written not by an expert, but an experienced beginner. I have begun many times and I have failed many times, but I still long to be a person of prayer; I still believe that prayer is the most important and the most natural thing that I can do.

This book is about praying through life. I believe the Christian faith is about being fully alive, and I believe prayer is the way we find this fullness. Praying through life means praying through the different stages of life. It means praying *with* children. It means praying *as* children. It means praying in the different circumstances of daily life. It means prayer in the home, at work, and wherever we happen to be. It is about prayer in the family. It is about praying on your own and praying with others. We only have one life; we must live it as God intended.

This book is quite unashamedly the shallow end of prayer, where we need others to help us. Wherever possible Christians should pray together, and when we pray our prayer should be simple and straightforward. Although there are many different ways of praying, and this book will try to deal with as many as seem relevant to the beginner, I am concerned that we approach the subject with a proper modesty of intention. The very word 'prayer' can elevate the subject, making it seem highbrow and difficult, beyond the reach of ordinary people. We used to talk of 'saying our prayers', and I feel for the beginner this is an altogether more suitable phrase. But it is not very fashionable. It is almost as if there is a movement in the Church that rather wants prayer to be an activity for the elite. We have a glut of spiritual 'experts' and an endless fascination with all sorts of different spiritualities, but what we don't have is simple teaching about saying prayers together in the home, at work or wherever we happen to be. This book seeks to redress the balance. If you are a 'spirituality junkie' I suggest you stop reading now. But if you have always found prayer difficult, or if you have never had any basic teaching about how to pray outside of the worshipping life of the Church, then please keep reading.

I believe that there are many people in our society today who already pray, and need that prayer to be formed by the mind of Christ and the lovely spiritual traditions of the Christian Church. I believe that there is plenty of help available. As we shall see, God himself not only longs for us with a passion that far surpasses our wistful yearning, but the heart of Christian prayer is his praying within us.

Jesus prays in me

'I cannot pray', said Henri Nouwen, 'but God can pray in me'[1] It took me a long while to learn this, and even so it is a truth I often forget, imagining prayer to be somehow dependent on my effort, or worse, my eloquence.

There is of course a paradox to prayer. It is all about the gift of God, and God praying in us, but it also has to be an act of human will. We are not machines kept going by God, we are free and we are responsible. The best way to understand this is in terms of call and response. God calls within every human heart, for he longs to make every human heart his dwelling. But he waits for us to respond. When we do, it is his delight to sing his song within us, and our voice, however faltering, and however unsure of the tune, is joined to the song of the Spirit and echoed by the saints and the angels.

I therefore know that although my prayer seems very small, I am beginning to hear God's song within me, and I am learning how to join in.

How I join in depends so much on who I am and the circumstances of my life. This book is to help you discover how you could be praying. It is not a book *about* prayer, although Part 1 does explain in some detail what prayer is, nor less is it a book *of* prayers, but a book to help you and your friends and your family and your church get started in the way of prayer.

'Pray the way you can, not the way you can't' is the well-known sensible advice of Dom Chapman. But often there is little help in discerning what this way might be, and this is especially the case if you have never really prayed at all, or if you have a family of small children, or if the schedules of your life are so hectic there seems no space to set aside for God, or in a hundred other situations that go to make up the reality of the Monday to Saturday life in which we must live our Christian vocation. How do you begin to pray in the ordinary circumstances of life? How do you find the way that you can pray? My prayer for this book is that it will help you find the answers to these questions.

I cannot give you the answer, because it will be different for every person, and it will change many times in every person's life, but I can take you on a journey through the basics of prayer and the basic ways in which we can begin praying.

Getting started

St Paul says 'Pray all the time' (1 Thessalonians 5.17). I do not think he means do that activity we call prayer all the time, but make your life a prayer: live the whole of your life in communion with God. In order for this to happen we will need times of prayer. We live in a world which thinks that 'doing things' is more important than 'saying prayers'. Even our churches are horrendously busy places and prayer is often relegated to the category of last resorts. As we shall see prayer is not an alternative to action, for, indeed, to pray is to *do something*. But neither is action an alternative to prayer. The spiritual writer Henri Nouwen puts it like this:

> *Prayer requires that we stand in God's presence with open hands, naked and vulnerable, proclaiming to ourselves and to others that without God we can do nothing.*

> Henri Nouwen, *Seeds of Hope*, p. 65.

Prayer should be our first concern, and the practical consequence will be trying to find a way of praying and a pattern of prayer that suits our situation, but prayer will lead to action, because God will be able to do so much through us.

What will these times of prayer be like? Well, they are very hard to describe. It's a bit like saying 'What is music?'. Words can only say so much; after a short while you have to say, 'Let me show you.' When you hear the music you understand what it is. And when you join in the making of the music, even if it is just singing and clapping your hands, you have an even greater understanding. But an explanation without a demonstration is a poor second best. It will be like this with prayer: hundreds of books have been written about it, but put them all together and they are not worth one moment of actual prayer.

And here am I writing another one! And here you are reading it! We both need to be clear about one thing: this book is only worth writing and only worth reading if it achieves two simple ends – to explain what prayer is actually about; and encourage people to start praying.

Therefore, if you have never really prayed, or if you have always found prayer difficult, do not wait till you get to the end of the book before you have another go. As soon as you find something which strikes a chord, put it into action. My words will only tell a fraction of the story. When you begin to unclench your fist and open your hands to God in prayer he will tell his story within you. And because our lives are all so different, it is important to keep fashioning what you read in a way that will be appropriate for your situation.

Part 2 – *Opening our hands to God* – deals with the practicalities of prayer. It begins with a chapter called 'First steps', and ends with one called 'Ten golden rules'. These will be particularly useful in helping you decide your best way of praying, and which other bits of the book are going to be the most relevant. There are chapters on all sorts of situations and ways of praying, and each contains practical ideas which relate to fairly broad categories of how we actually live our lives.

A lot of the emphasis is on family prayer and prayer in the home. I need to say why this is with reference to my own spiritual journey. Most of what I have learned about prayer has come through my experience of being a parent, not my experience of being a priest, though of course the two overlap.

For the first six years of married life, except in emergency and the occasional hurried grace before meals, my wife and I rarely prayed together. Yet as a priest of the Church of England I tried each day to say those prayers which form the office of the Church and tried to find some space for personal prayer. The trouble was that church and home had become separated – no prayer life at home with my wife, but a huge prayer life at work in church! In my ministry I regularly spoke to people about the importance of prayer, but had failed to translate that into the patterns of my own daily life. I exhorted people to pray, but was not able to commend appropriate patterns that would be rooted in people's daily experience. Prayer for me had become private and professional. I either prayed on my own, or in the context of my particular ministry.

Looking back I am also able to see that part of the reason why this happened is that no one had ever taught me much about the simple daily prayer that I am commending here. I knew a lot about the mountain tops of prayer (through reading rather than experience I hasten to add!) but hardly anything about the foothills where most of us spend most of our lives. I thought prayer had to be tremendously deep or tremendously exciting. I did not know about the ordinary life of shared prayer.

All this changed when I became a parent. When our first child was born, like all parents I was struck by the awesome responsibility of bringing another human being into the world and of helping that person grow to maturity. This would involve many challenges, none of which I had been much prepared for, but in particular I considered my responsibility as a Christian parent. I wanted my children to grow up in the Christian faith. I wanted them to share that faith. I wanted them to know about the reality of God, not as a second-hand idea, but as a first-hand experience. It was pretty obvious that this wondrous task needed to involve rather more than teaching them *about* the Christian faith. I wanted them to grow up knowing God (not just knowing about God), and I wanted this to feel natural and ordinary (because it is).

What God was challenging me to see was that prayer, the prayer that I had allowed to become either private or professional, was the way to get to this experience. Prayer could shape the lives of my children and show them the reality of God. It would have to be shared prayer: something which clearly indicated what we as a family believed life to be about. It would have to be simple prayer: we are talking about small children here. But by praying together in the home we could let God claim his place at the centre of family life. This would be good in itself, but it would also be the way in which children could grow up in the faith, and experience it as a lived reality.

I pray in Jesus

I now have three children and family prayer each day is an integral part of our life together. Prayer-time, as we call it, is as normal a part of family life as mealtime and bathtime and playtime. This has radically changed family life and has steadily, but no less radically, changed my understanding of prayer. It is from this experience that I now want to encourage and teach the Church in simple patterns of praying together. I have a particular concern for families, and large sections of the practical parts of this book are directed towards their needs. But what I learned in the home – that prayer is central to life; that we need to pray together; that prayer need not be complicated – is relevant to everyone.

However, many of us do not live our lives in families, and even within families it is wrong to assume everyone shares the Christian faith. Therefore there are specific ideas for couples, and for single people, and ideas for praying in the work place as well as at home. And there are many overlaps. We all have some experience of family, and at some part of our life all of us are single. I hope it will be possible to use the different ideas to form the basis of regular prayer for people in every situation.

But it is also wise to remember that we are all part of the family of God. When he looks at us, all he sees is small children. And all the while I was trying to be so grown up with God, my fist was tightly clenched. I was relying on myself; I was thinking I was in control. Praying with small children has helped a great deal. I can feel the muscles in my hands beginning to relax.

The children's leader at our church recently commented to me, 'How come most prayers that adults say begin with please, and most prayers children say begin with thank you?' This is a fascinating observation. The child's relationship with God is so trusting and so thankful that it can liberate our prayer also to be simple, trusting and thankful. I am even beginning to open my empty hands to God. Thus I have started to take the journey that Jesus demands, saying that if we are to enter the kingdom we must become like little children (see Mark 10.14-15). There is great irony here: the world spends its time trying to turn children into adults, and Jesus spends his time trying to turn adults into children.

I am greatly encouraged by the writings of Thérèse of Lisieux. Her path to God is known as 'the little way', and it is full of encouragement to beginners. She writes:

I've always wished that I could be a saint. But whenever I compare myself to the Saints there was always this unfortunate difference – they were like great mountains, hiding their heads in the clouds, and I was only an insignificant grain of sand, trodden down by all who passed by. However, I wasn't going to be discouraged; I said to myself: 'God wouldn't inspire us with ambitions that can't be realised. Obviously there's nothing great to be made of me, so it must be possible for me to aspire to sanctity in spite of my insignificance. I've got to take myself just as I am, with all my imperfections; but somehow I shall have to find a little way all of my own, which will be a direct short cut to heaven. After all (I said to myself) we live in an age of inventions. Nowadays, people don't even bother to climb the stairs – rich people, anyhow; they find a lift more convenient. Can't I find a lift which will take me up to Jesus, since I'm not big enough to climb the steep stairway to perfection?' So I looked in the Bible for some hint about the life I wanted, and I came across the passage where Eternal Wisdom says: 'Is anyone simple as a little child? Then let him come to me' To that Wisdom I went; it seemed as if I was on the right track; what did God undertake to do for the child-like soul that responded to his invitation? I read on, and this is what I found: 'I shall console you like a mother caressing her son; you shall be like children carried at the breast, fondled on a mother's lap' Never were words so touching: never was such music to rejoice the heart – I could, after all, be lifted up to heaven, in the arms of Jesus! And if that was to happen, there was no need for me to grow bigger; on the contrary, I must be as small as ever, smaller than ever.

Thérèse of Lisieux, *Autobiography of a Saint*, pp. 194–5.

In the very act of writing this book, I must reluctantly admit that I have not progressed very far, searching for the stairs before allowing God to lift me up. But what Thérèse does help us to see is that progress in the life of prayer is not about what we achieve, but what we allow ourselves to receive. This will mean discipline – we need an act of will to open up our hands to God – but it will also be a work of grace, God's love melting and shaping us. And as with all things, it is much, much better to have begun, than never to have started.

Part 1

What is prayer?
Unclenching the fist

The Lord Jesus Himself will teach you how you should pray.
He is the creative Word which you may receive in the silence
of your heart and the fruitful soil of your life.

Rule for a New Brother, p.33.

1

Prayer is relationship with God

The whole reason why we pray is summed up in the sight and vision of him to whom we pray' the more the soul sees God, the more by his grace does it want him.

Julian of Norwich, *Revelations of Divine Love*, p. 129.

H uman beings are made for relationship with God. 'I worship, therefore I am,'[1] proclaims Bishop Michael Marshall in rebuke to all those other half truths which diminish and reduce the human spirit. I pray, therefore I am. When we pray we discover the truth about ourselves that we are children of God. Within this relationship we can flourish and become fully ourselves as God intended us to be. This is not the only way to be happy – clearly the world has many happy and fulfilled people who are not Christians – but that fullness we long for only comes from God, because everything which is good and fulfilling ultimately comes from him. He is the source of life and the joys we find in every human endeavour flow from his creating heart. Therefore, when we seek the heart of God in prayer, we are seeking the deepest joy of all, and the deepest fulfilment. We discover the reality of God not as a new truth, but as the most brilliant expression of all the truths we have ever known, for nothing which is good is outside the heart of God. When we pray we come to the peak of the mountain in whose foothills we have always played.

Prayer is the most natural thing in the world. It can also be the hardest. Because it is relationship it is about letting go and allowing someone else to be at the centre of your life. In so many ways the human spirit will recoil from this kind of loving. We like to be at the centre ourselves.

But this is the most fundamental truth about Christian prayer. Prayer is relationship with God; it is the relationship we are made for. Like all relationships it is not easy to describe. I know what it feels like to be in love, but it is hard to define it. Put together all the most beautiful love poems in the world and they are as nothing compared with a few moments of love itself.

Being a Christian is like a love affair. In Jesus we see how God gives himself to us in love.

'Love one another, as I have loved you', says Jesus. 'No one can have greater love than to lay down his life for his friends' (John 15.12-13).

I am a Christian not because I know a lot of things *about* God, but because I *know* God. I am in this relationship. It is Jesus who has made this possible. Jesus shows me the reality of God, that God is not just an interesting idea, but a loving, creating and sustaining presence, upholding all the universe and available to me personally. In Jesus we can know God with the same intimacy with which a child knows a father.

This does not mean I do not have my doubts and anxieties, but it does mean that life now has a new perspective. What was once a journey – the human life travelling from birth to death – is now a pilgrimage, a journey home. I now believe that God is the source of all life; that my life comes from him and will return to him. The living God is like a fifth dimension permeating all reality and sustaining every moment.

You may have noticed how nearly all Christian prayers end with a formula like, 'through Jesus Christ our Lord', or 'in the name of Christ'. These words express this basic truth. We come to God through Jesus. 'I am the way to the Father,' says Jesus in John's gospel (John 14.6). In the name of Jesus, we have access to God.

This relationship, which God has initiated through his love, is something we enter freely. God will never force his way into our lives. He loves us too much and wants only the free response of our love. But the great paradox of this relationship is that when we put Jesus at the centre of our life, he puts us at the centre of his.

Like all relationships, it needs to be worked at. It is through worship and prayer that the relationship is nurtured and sustained. Prayer is the personal dimension of this life of communion with God. Worship is the corporate dimension. We need both: 'communal and individual prayer belong together as two folded hands'.[2]

Beginning the relationship

If you are a convinced Christian then you will probably not need to be persuaded of the idea of faith equalling relationship. If, however, you are one of those many thousands of people who are on a spectrum spanning from half-committed faith to half-hearted unbelief, not really sure what you think or what you believe, then understanding faith as relationship is probably the key to spiritual progress. This has certainly been the case in my experience.

If you want to get to know someone there is only so far you can go by reading about them, looking at pictures, asking other people's opinions. Eventually the only way to get to know them is to meet them. This is when knowing *about* someone starts to change to actually *knowing* them. 'Knowledge of' becomes 'relationship with'. It will be like this with God.

> *If we think knowing God is very different from knowing other people,*
> *then we are trying to do something for which we have no equipment*
> *and very little natural ability.*

George Guiver, Everyday God, p. 8.

This is something which is not very often said about prayer. We think it is something difficult. We imagine that God is like an elusive wavelength on the radio. We know he is there somewhere but we just can't tune in. But the point is this: knowing God *is* like knowing other people because God has made himself known to us in Jesus Christ. We *do* have all the equipment we need and all the ability necessary. We just need to find the way of praying that is right for us.

Prayer is the way we meet God. Putting it bluntly like that is quite frightening: not least because a lot of the time it doesn't feel as inspiring as this short sentence might suggest. But there it is, this is the truth about prayer. Prayer is meeting God. The only way to find out if this is true is to begin praying. Many have compared this first stage of prayer to swimming. It may not look as if the water will hold the weight of your body: the evidence of that brick you just threw in seems to suggest otherwise; but there we are, some people say it is possible to swim. How do you find out? Well, you jump in the water.

But this is the trouble with so much teaching about prayer. You are exhorted to jump in at the deep end. Prayer often seems to be presented as this highly esoteric activity – long periods of deep contemplation – or an emotionally charged activity – always inspired and always inspiring. This just depresses me. I have not had these experiences. It is not that these understandings of prayer are not important, but they are styles of prayer which do not suit every person, and they are ways of prayer that most of us gradually develop into. But there are other ways of learning to pray just as there are other ways of learning to swim. There is the shallow end, and there are arm bands and there are swimming instructors. We need the same simple teaching about prayer.

To find this we need to look into the DNA of the Church. Here there is a deep-rooted tradition, stretching back to the experience of the first Christians, and shaped by the Jewish practice of making the home the centre of worshipping life, of saying set prayers together wherever you happened to be. This is a largely unrecognised, and rather unfashionable, tradition of Christian prayer, but it is probably of much greater value to thousands of ordinary Christians. It *is the plain idea of people saying prayers together*. This can happen in the home or wherever people find themselves in their everyday Monday to Saturday life. But it is about *praying together*, since we need help, instruction and encouragement in our prayer.

God is relationship

Perhaps the greatest encouragement we can find in the relationship of prayer is the knowledge that God himself is relationship. The God we pray to is a community of persons: Father, Son and Holy Spirit. When we pray we enter into that relationship of love which is the very nature of God.

Prayer together in this way is also about re-discovering confidence in set patterns of prayer and in the power and meaning of ritual. This will begin with longing for God – we will say more about this later on – just as human relationships often begin with longing for another person. It will be nurtured and sustained by little patterns and rituals, just like in human relationships. When your spouse or lover says to you 'Do you love me?', it is no good saying, 'Of course I do', you must actually say the words 'I love you!' The longing needs to be expressed. This is all that growing in prayer means. Although this book is not going to go much beyond the most basic early stages of a life of prayer, even those heights of mystical experience which some Christians have described are best understood as the joys of the lover being with his beloved. In mature human relationships some of us will have experienced just how good it is to be in someone's presence, not having to say a word, just cherishing the one you love. Those forms of prayer known as meditation and contemplation are like this.

But let us come down from the mountains and return to base camp. George Guiver, in his wonderful little book *Everyday Prayer*, speaks of prayer as ritual conversation. Just as human relationships cannot be lived in a state of perpetual intensity, nor can our relationship with God. Just as human relationships develop and are sustained by little rituals and patterns, so will our relationship with God. In small ways and in regular and familiar patterns we will discover different ways to pray. We will discover that prayer can be ordinary and natural and we will be able to find the way of praying that is right for us.

Anthony de Mello tells the story of a bishop whose ship stops at a remote island for a day. He comes across three fishermen who he is surprised to find are Christians. 'Do you know the Lord's Prayer?' he asks them quizzically. He is shocked to discover they do not. 'How do you pray, then?' he asks. They reply, 'We lift our eyes to heaven and we say, "We are three, you are three, have mercy on us."' Appalled at the primitive nature of their prayer, and wanting to use his time on the island as profitably as possible, he sets about teaching them. They are poor learners but by the time the bishop's boat sails the next day he has the satisfaction of hearing them recite the Lord's Prayer all the way through.

Months later the bishop's boat again passes by the island. As he is saying his evening prayers, the bishop recalls with pleasure how his patient efforts had taught those three fishermen how to pray. As he is thinking this he notices a small light approaching the boat from the island. As he watches, the light gets bigger and bigger. In amazement the bishop sees the three fishermen walking on the water towards him. As they get within speaking distance they call out to him: 'Bishop!' they exclaim. 'We saw your boat going by and we have hurried out to see you.'

'What do you want?' replies the awe-struck bishop. 'bishop,' they say, 'We are so sorry. We have forgotten your lovely prayer. We say "Our father in heaven, hallowed be your name, your kingdom come . . ." but then we forget. Please tell us the prayer again.' The bishop is humbled. 'Go back to your homes, my friends', he says to them, 'and each time you pray, say, "We are three, you are three, have mercy on us".'[3]

2

Prayer is relationship with others

It is all one great dance . . . I am praying by myself . . . Jesus is pray-
ing in me. So is the Holy Spirit . . . The saints are singing their
eternal song . . . Above all, it is the endless, love-filled prayer of the
Holy Trinity which sweeps us up into its movement . . .

George Guiver, *Everyday God,* p.39.

When the disciples asked Jesus to teach them how to pray he gave them a simple formula. He said, 'When you pray, this is what to say' (Luke 11.2), and then he taught them what we now know as the Lord's Prayer. Unlike the three fishermen in Anthony de Mello's story, our problem with this prayer is not difficulty in remembering it, but over-familiarity. We have probably said and heard the Lord's Prayer so many times that we are in danger of becoming immune to its charms.

But the point I want to make here is that Jesus gave his disciples a simple prayer for them to memorise and say. He did not exhort them to spend hours in meditation, nor did he expect them always to be able to express prayer in their own words. Of course he longed that they would grow in that same intimacy of relationship with God that we see exemplified in his own ministry, but his first priority was to give them a prayer that would be the foundation and the heart of all prayer.

Jesus teaches us to pray

It is worth, then, taking a good look at this most fundamental of Christian prayers. It will teach us just about everything we need to know. It will show us the truth of our basic assertion about prayer – that prayer is relationship with God. It will also show us how prayer is relationship with others.

Just the first word has an enormous amount to teach us. The first word is 'our'. The Lord's Prayer is a corporate prayer. It does not say, 'My Father in heaven', but 'Our Father'. It does not say, 'Give *me* today *my* daily bread'; but 'Give us *our* bread'. It does not say 'Forgive *me* my sins; lead *me* not into temptation', but, 'Forgive us *our* sins, lead *us* not into temptation'.

If we were to change the Lord's Prayer from the third person to the first, it would not just diminish the prayer, it would destroy it. A prayer of mutual generosity would become one of narrow selfishness. We are not isolated individuals concerned only for our own welfare. Through our baptism we belong to one another and we belong to God. Paul describes the Church as Christ's body. Just as in a human body one part cannot say to another, 'I have no need of you', so it is in the Church. 'If one part is hurt', says Paul, 'all the parts share its pain. And if one part is honoured, all the parts share its joy' (1 Corinthians 12.16).

It is abhorrent to say 'My Father', without recognising that God is the Father of all people. He cannot be my Father unless he is first our Father. Likewise it is abhorrent to ask that I may have my daily bread, and my sins forgiven, without first recognising my common humanity: that we all need our daily bread; that we all need the grace of God's forgiveness.

Praying together

There is no such thing as private prayer! What I mean by this is that when we pray (even if we happen to be physically on our own) we are caught up in something much bigger than ourselves.

When we pray we are in solidarity with Christian people everywhere

Within the body of the Church we are supported and encouraged by each other's prayers. At any one time when you sit down to say your prayers there are countless millions of Christian people all around the world who are also praying. You probably cannot hear them; you may feel very isolated in your own faith, perhaps because it is not shared by your family and your friends, but the truth remains: you are not alone.

We need also to remember that time does not exist for God. In God's eternity all prayer is one. Even if you were the only Christian person left in the whole world, still you would not be alone. To God a thousand years are like a single day (2 Peter 3.8): the voice of your prayer is joined by the voices of Christian people who have gone before us.

When we pray the Holy Spirit prays within us

Our prayers are joined to the prayers of Jesus to the Father. This has a very practical application. Many people find prayer difficult precisely because they believe it to be private. They believe it to be something which is primarily dependent upon their own effort and ability. But the deepest truth about Christian prayer is that when we pray it is actually not us but the Holy Spirit praying in us. 'When we cry, "Abba, Father!" it is the Spirit himself bearing witness with our spirit that we are children of God,' says St Paul (Romans 8.15-16).

The prayer of the Church on earth (that's us!) is joined to the prayer of the Church in heaven

When we pray, the song of our prayer – or, I should say, the song the Holy Spirit sings within us – is joined to the music of the saints and the angels.

I remember many years ago preparing to celebrate a mid-week Eucharist on a cold and snowy winter's night. Usually we would have a congregation of ten or twelve people. On this night only one person turned up. She poked her head round the sacristy door, just before the service was about to begin, and said, 'Oh, don't worry just for me'. I replied, kindly but also firmly, 'I am not doing this just for you! This is the prayer of the Church. We are surrounded by a great cloud of witnesses; we are in solidarity with Christian communities all over the world who are also gathering to celebrate the Eucharist, and anyway, the church is not empty, it is full of angels! Whatever made you think you were the only one here!'

Of course it doesn't *feel* like this most of the time, but this does not make it any less true. And whenever the Eucharist is offered the truth that the prayer of the Church on earth is united with the prayer of the Church in heaven is affirmed when the priest says, 'Therefore with angels and archangels and with all the company of heaven, we proclaim your great and glorious name, forever praising you and saying . . .' And then we all join in a hymn of praise to God, 'Holy, holy, holy, Lord God of power and might, heaven and earth are full of your glory.' (ASB, p. 131).

Get it? Heaven *and* earth. That is the scandalous truth of the Christian faith. The glory of the Lord fills the whole of creation. God is not confined to the heavens; he is available to us on earth.

The Christian life can be very personal, but it can never be private. But this is precisely how many people see it. They want their own private relationship with God: they readily talk about *my* faith and *my* prayers. We must vigorously challenge this view, otherwise the whole Christian faith is reduced to a private option with no claim upon the whole of life. In fact the very word 'private' comes from the Latin verb *privo* which means to steal! The Christian life is corporate and public, and whenever we imagine that being a Christian is just about me and God, we rob the Christian faith of its true catholicity.

There is no 'my' with God. It is always, as the beginning of the Lord's Prayer affirms, 'our'.

3

Prayer is relationship *for* God

Sometimes when the heart is dry . . . reason and grace drive us to cry aloud to our Lord, recalling his blessed passion and great goodness. And the strength of our Lord's word comes to the soul, and fires the heart, and leads it by grace into its real business, enabling it to pray happily and to enjoy our Lord in truth. Thanksgiving is a blessed thing in his sight.

Julian of Norwich, *Revelations of Divine Love*, p.125.

The second word of the Lord's Prayer is as dramatic as the first. Jesus calls God 'Father'. For the Jews at the time of Jesus this would have been quite unusual. They would have spoken of God as their king, but if they did call God Father they would be referring to God as the Father of their nation. The actual word Jesus uses is *Abba*. This is even more shocking. This is the word a little child would use. It would be best translated into English as 'Daddy'. Jesus, therefore, addresses God with a radical intimacy that was almost unknown up to this point. And as if this isn't enough, he encourages this intimacy in his disciples. 'If you know me, you will know my Father too', says Jesus (John 14.7). 'Anything you ask in my name, the Father will give you' (John 15.16).

When we pray we need to develop this same intimacy. This will not always be easy. Many of us feel embarrassed about prayer; we do not know what to say, we feel tongue-tied and uncomfortable. Some of us have had bad experiences of fathers and mothers, so it is not an image which conjures up the feelings of love and security I am describing. Even so we can gain comfort from Jesus' assertion that if we have seen him, we have seen the Father (John 14.9). In other words, if you want to know what God is like, then look at Jesus. It is not just that Jesus calls God Father; his own example of love and service shows what kind of parent God is. In this sense God is both Father and Mother, and to know God as he has been revealed in Jesus will not only help us to come to God with intimacy, but also heal the wounds of the difficult relationships we may have had with our own fathers and mothers.

Longing for God

Calling God Father also defines the essential child-likeness of all Christian faith. We have already spoken about Jesus proclaiming that the greatest in the kingdom will have to be like little children (Mark 9.36), but this aspect of his teaching highlights an attitude to prayer that is rarely emphasised enough: prayer as *being*. It is good for the little child to be in the presence of his parent. 'I hold myself in quiet and silence, like a little child in its mother's arms,' says the psalmist (Psalm 131.2).

Prayer in its simplest form is being with God and resting in his presence. It is also longing and desire. It is wanting God. I am so aware that much of my own prayer is still like this. I long for God. I want God, and, to borrow a phrase from Michael Ramsey, 'I *want* to want God.'¹ There is a danger that this longing can become introverted and selfish, but at its heart it is wholesome and good. Peter, in his own restlessness when many others were leaving Jesus, says to him, 'To whom shall we go? You have the message of eternal life' (John 6.69).

'You created me for Yourself', writes Augustine, 'and my heart is restless until it rests in you.' And describing his conversion to the Christian faith, Augustine expresses himself in terms of desire:

> You called and cried to me and broke open my deafness: and you sent forth your beams and shone upon me and chased away my blindness: you breathed fragrance upon me, and I drew in my breath and do now pant for you: I tasted you, and now I hunger and thirst for you: you touched me, and I have burned for your peace.

St Augustine of Hippo, *Confessions*, Book 10.27.

The psalms are also full of the same sensuous language as the human spirit craves for God:

> As a deer yearns for running streams,
> so I yearn for you, my God (Psalm 42.1-2).

> *God, you are my God, I pine for you;*
> *my heart thirsts for you,*
> *my body longs for you,*
> *as a land parched, dreary and waterless* (Psalm 63.1).

I am sure that this is where many people are with prayer. They want to pray and they want to know God, but they don't know what to do next. Rather than feeling guilty about this sense of longing, rest in the knowledge that you are already praying. God is your Father. He made you and he loves you, and the longing you feel in your own heart is the yearning of your spirit to find communion with the living God. It is the beginning of prayer, and even in the most barren periods of our life it is a form of prayer we return to. Wanting God and wanting to want him.

I read in the newspapers recently about one family discovering prayer in a time of great need and anxiety. The footballer Alan Hudson was hit by a car while walking home. He battled for his life during a fourteen-hour operation as surgeons worked to remove a blood clot from his brain. This is what his son said to the journalists: 'Me and my family sat in the chapel praying to God, in my case for the first time in my life.' And he added, 'He is not fully recovered, but they have stabilised the bleeding.' His former team mate, Malcolm Macdonald, said, 'It is a time for praying and that is what I will be doing.'

This type of prayer surges from the human spirit. It is very natural, and it is a direct expression of our love. It cries out with anguish and longing. We pour out our heart to God. This is very good. It is what Hannah is doing when the priest Eli mistakenly thinks she is drunk. 'I have not been drinking' she replies, 'I am pouring my soul out to the Lord . . . I am speaking to him from the depth of my grief' (1 Samuel 1.15-16).

Honouring God

It is in the context of this longing, which proceeds from our parent–child relationship with God, that we can say prayer is *for* God. And this is echoed in the next three phrases of the Lord's Prayer. They are all about what we can give to God. This may seem an impertinent question. What could we possibly give to God? But prayer is not just about what we ask from God – this is a common misunderstanding – it is about what God asks from us.

Well, first of all God wants our love. For it to be love it must be freely given. This is the nature of the Christian relationship which we have already described. What then could we wish for God after we have claimed that relationship of love by saying he is 'Our Father'? This is how the Lord's Prayer proceeds:

> *Hallowed be your name,*
> *your kingdom come,*
> *your will be done,*
> *in earth as in heaven.*

What the Lord's Prayer desires is that God's name be honoured by all who bear it; that his rule may prevail; and that his loving purpose take effect, on earth as it already does in heaven. These are the things we wish for God. Prayer is for God because in prayer we give our will to God. We make his name holy in our lives; we commit ourselves to the establishment of his kingdom; we submit to his will.

Seeking his will

This is probably the hardest bit of all – praying 'Your will be done'. And it is the hinge-phrase in the Lord's Prayer as we turn from desiring things for God, to asking things for the world and for ourselves. But the context of our asking is that God's will should prevail.

Prayer is relationship with God for others

Prayer is the way to both the heart of God and the heart of the world — precisely because they have been joined through the suffering of Christ'. Praying is letting one's own heart become the place where the tears of God and the tears of God's children can merge and become tears of hope.

Henri Nouwen, *Seeds of Hope*, p.68.

I n the Garden of Gethsemane on the night of his arrest Jesus struggled to accept and live by the Father's will. Jesus prayed, '*Abba*, Father, for you everything is possible. Take this cup away from me. But let it be as you, not I, would have it' (Mark 14.36).

We need to remind ourselves of this: if it was hard for Jesus then, of course it will be hard for us.

But we should ask for things from God. We know that he loves us and we should be bold in making our requests. And we should expect that God will hear and answer our prayer. Not always when we want, or how we want — there is the story of the man who prayed for flowers, and God sent him a spade and a packet of seeds! — but Jesus has told us to ask.

> *Ask, and it will be given to you; search, and you will find; knock and the door will be opened to you* (Matthew 7.7).

In fact, a lot of the teaching about prayer in the gospels centres around asking for things. This is not the heart of prayer — that is relationship with God — but if the relationship is one of parent to child, what could be more natural than asking?

It is like this in family life: children have ready access to their parents. My children do not have to make an appointment to see me. It is not always convenient when they burst into the room demanding attention, and sometimes they will have to be told to wait, and sometimes what they want is not good for them and will have to be withheld; but I will not turn them away. They can always have my time and my attention. There will never be a situation when they are not my children and I am not their father. Their access to me and my readiness to give myself to them define our relationship. This is not always easy – in fact it is exhausting trying to meet the demands of small children – but I do not want it any other way. I never want them to think they cannot turn to me.

It is like this with God. Julian of Norwich puts it beautifully:

> *The love of God Most High for our soul is so wonderful that it surpasses all knowledge. No created thing can know the greatness, the sweetness, the tenderness of the love that our Maker has for us. By his grace and help therefore let us in spirit stand and gaze, eternally marvelling at the supreme, surpassing, single-minded, incalculable love that God, who is goodness, has for us. Then we can ask reverently of our lover whatever we will.*

Julian of Norwich, *Revelations of Divine Love*, pp. 70-1.

Intercession

We call these asking prayers *intercession*. Jesus' own ministry includes many such prayers: he asks forgiveness for those who crucify him; for Peter's faith to be increased; for his disciples to be sanctified; for the unity of his fledgling Church; and, as we have just seen, for his own faithfulness to God's will.

Like Jesus, we too should ask things of God. The difference between our intercessions and those of Jesus, is that all Jesus' prayer echoes the will of the Father. This will not always be the case with our prayers.

The Lord's Prayer asks for three things in particular:

> *Give us today our daily bread.*
> *Forgive us our sins as we forgive those who sin against us.*
> *Lead us not into temptation but deliver us from evil.*

These requests are simple and basic, they flow from the heart of God. We are instructed to ask for the provision of material need; forgiveness for ourselves and a forgiving heart towards others; to be spared from trials beyond our strength and given protection from evil'.

In this way we can see that the pattern of the Lord's Prayer is three praises followed by three petitions, or as Austin Farrer put it in a wonderful little homily he preached on the Lord's Prayer 'three hearty wishes and three humble requests.'[1]

We should ask God for things, and no request is too small, but we should always be asking that God's will be done, not ours. We should follow the example of Mary, the Lord's mother. She prayed, 'I am the Lord's servant, let it happen to me as you have said' (Luke 1.38). She is able to abandon herself to God's will. This does not mean she did not ask things of God, but what she desired more than anything, even when it seemed that what God was wanting was so impossible, was that his will be done in her life. 'Do whatever he tells you', she says to the servants at the wedding feast at Cana, and they follow Jesus' instructions and the stone jars of water are miraculously turned to wine (John 2.5).

Intercession is not about persuading God to do something that is opposed to his will, but standing in God's presence on behalf of another person and seeking God's will for that person's life. Our job is to fill the jars with water. We must then trust God to do the rest, in his time, and in his way, and for the fulfilment of his will. God is concerned for all people and for the whole of life. Nothing has its being except through him (Colossians 1.17). Jesus even says that every hair on our head is counted and that not one sparrow falls to the ground without the Father knowing (Matthew 10.29-30).

We should therefore have no reluctance in asking things of God. He is our Father. He cares for us and wants what is best for us. We are worth so much more than many sparrows! He also *knows* what is best for us. In the same passage where Jesus invites us to ask things of God, he also says, 'What Father among you would give his son a stone when he asked for bread?' (Matthew 7.9). Well, many times we ask things of God and we do not seem to get what we request. The trouble is that we think we are asking for bread, but actually we are asking for a stone. We do not know what is best. We would not give our own children sweets all the time, however much they begged us. The sweets would destroy their teeth. We know it is best if they go without. Too often we may be asking God for things which would destroy us. Sometimes God is saying no. Sometimes he is saying wait.

Always there is the challenge in the Christian life to love the things that God has given us. Anthony de Mello tells the story of the man who wanted to rid his lawn of dandelions. He tried everything, but still they plagued him. Eventually he wrote to an eminent horticulturist, listing all the things that he had tried. 'What shall I do now?' the letter ended. The reply came back: 'I suggest you learn to love them.'[2]

The mystery of prayer

Intercession is not magic. When we pray we are not asking God to cast a spell. But neither is the whole of life pre-programmed. Things can change for the better, or for the worse. God has made us free. Free to accept his will, free to reject it. We have control over our lives. We are not puppets being controlled or manipulated by God. We can influence events. Intercession is not a technique for changing God's mind, but it is a releasing of power as we place ourselves in a relationship of co-operation with God. When we pray we are in communion with God, we seek his will and the channels of communication are open. We are available to God and he will work through us.

There is no real distinction, then, between prayer and action. Prayer *is* action, because God's energy is released into a situation. Prayer *leads* to action because we cannot with integrity pray for something which we are not also prepared to do something about.

Many Christians fail in this respect. We pray for the suffering of the world, but most of us will spend more money each week on newspapers to read about that suffering than we will give in charity to alleviate it. But to pray 'your kingdom come, your will be done' commits us to the values of God, and should bring us openly to challenge so many of the ingrained habits of our culture which are far removed from the gospel.

By all means let us pray for family and friends and our own needs, but let us not be trivial in our prayer. Always be seeking the mind of God: praying for those people and causes which are closest to God's heart, and then let that prayer make a difference in the life we lead.

We are back with Jesus in Gethsemane. We would rather this cup was taken away. Prayer takes us into dangerous places. It commits us to act. When we ask, we are asking that God's will be done in our lives. When we search, we are searching out God's way of love and justice. The door on which we knock is the door to the kingdom of heaven.

The mystery of suffering

We also need to be mindful that sometimes things happen which clearly are not of God's will. We pray for wars to cease, for starving children to be fed, for illness to be healed, and our prayers seem to go unanswered. It would be unspeakable to say that these are the will of God, it is just that we cannot see it. It would be equally unspeakable to say that we have not prayed properly, or hard enough. How, then, can we make sense of the terrible suffering in the world and still presume to believe a loving God hears our prayer?

This is the hardest bit of all. Hard, because we all know suffering in our life. Hard, because the one time we all pray is when those we love are suffering.

I won't pretend I have an easy answer. But it would be wrong for a book about prayer to avoid this most basic of questions. If prayer does not do any good when someone is suffering then can anything we have said here about prayer and about God be real?

Before I was ordained I worked for a year in St Christopher's Hospice in South London. I witnessed some amazing things there. But the saddest sight I saw was some earnest Christians praying around the bed of someone who was dying, exhorting God to return him to his former health. They had misunderstood the whole journey of life, and at the very point when we must pray for the grace to let go of this life, they were frantically clinging on as if this life were all there is.

The prayer that was needed at that point was the prayer of abandonment that Jesus made to the Father on the cross: 'Into your hands I place my spirit' (Luke 23.46). Their prayer was the wrong prayer because they were asking for what they wanted, and had shut out the voice of God. He was calling their friend home. Of course it is natural to want those we love to be returned to health, but we must also hope that at the hour of death, both for our loved ones and ourselves, we may be able to discern the approach of death and greet it as a friend. Not only was the prayer I witnessed putting God to the test, it was very nearly a denial of the gospel, for out of death comes life. And at the human level the insistence that God would make the person better denied everyone around the bedside the chance to say good-bye, make amends and say last things to one another.

In times of suffering we need to place those we love in God's hands. We need to believe that he knows what is best for them. We also need to take comfort from the suffering and death of Jesus. His passion and crucifixion show us that God is with us in our suffering and at the hour of our death. Jesus has two names that bear testimony to this: Emmanuel, which means God is with us, and Jesus, which means God saves. He is our comforter as well as our redeemer but often we will experience him as Emmanuel, the God who is with us, before we will experience him as Jesus, the God who saves.

We do not know why there is so much suffering in the world. Much of it is made by our own selfish rejection of the way of God – our greed, and spite and envy. But much of it just seems to be there in creation – illness and disaster and eventually death. All we can say is that in Jesus, God is not dispassionately removed from all this, but passionately involved. At the hour of his suffering he placed himself in God's hands. We must follow his example.

I have placed people in God's hands in this way and miraculously seen people restored to health. I have placed people in God's hands and seen them receive fresh courage and strength to endure. I have placed people in God's hands and have seen them die. What I have stopped believing is that it is my fault if things don't turn out as I want them to. There are many aspects of God's will that it is impossible for me to understand. There are also many things which happen in this life which are just plain contrary to his will, many of them a direct result of our fascination with evil.

But our God is a redeemer. Even death has no hold over him. In the midst of our suffering we need to see the final triumph of the cross. This does not make the pain any less painful, but it does place human tragedy in the proper context of God's ultimate victory. What we need to look for in the healing, in the endurance, in the suffering and in the dying, is the saving passion of Jesus. And through the power of the cross we must pray for all these things – for healing, for perseverance, for deliverance from evil, for strength in suffering and for a happy death.

Again, we see why there is so much to be learned from the example of Mary. Her faithfulness to the will of God enabled her to come to the foot of the cross when most of the other disciples had fled. She was able to see the unfolding of God's purpose, even in the midst of pain.

Suffering will not always show us God's purpose. Often it will show us the opposite. But the suffering of Jesus does show us that God is involved.

I remember my first day at St Christopher's Hospice. A woman whose name I do not remember, and whom I never saw again, beckoned me to her bedside and, guessing I was a new boy, told me not to be afraid. It was wonderful that in her last few hours of life she could reach out to me, a stranger but a fellow pilgrim, and offer me comfort. It was supposed to be the other way around, but she had sensed my anxiety. When I had arrived on the ward that morning all I had seen was cancer. Not people, but illness. Now she showed me the people beneath the pain, the true humanity within the suffering.

It was an autumn day and watching the leaves drifting in the wind she likened what was left of her life to the last few leaves falling from a tree. But she was not downcast. Sad, yes, because the summer was over. But confident: she believed in the spring.

She died later that day. But she taught me what it means to unite our suffering with the suffering of Christ. She taught me what it means to die a Christian death.

The mystery of love

This points us to the final thing I want to say about prayer. Prayer is love. The passion of Jesus shows us the depths and purpose of God's love for us. This love is so hard to describe. It is echoed in all human loving, and when we experience the pain of bereavement we find out more about its mystery. For although we long for the pain to be healed, we would rather it stay, for if the pain went away so would the love. It is because we love so much that we hurt so much. I never fail to be moved by the writings of Julian of Norwich as she describes her visions of Jesus. She wonderfully affirms that the heart of the gospel is love: the love that is made possible through his passion and death.

In prayer we enter into this great mystery of love, for in prayer the human soul is united to God. In prayer our communion is with the whole creation and we are very close to loved ones who have died. Julian describes her vision of the heart of Jesus, 'riven in two' a place, fair and delightful, large enough for all saved mankind to rest in peace and love.' With her we can hear him speak to us:

> *'See, how I have loved you.' As if to say, 'My dearest, look at your Lord, your God, your Maker, and your endless joy. See the delight I have in your salvation; and because you love me, rejoice with me.'*

Julian of Norwich, *Revelations of Divine Love*, p. 100.

5

A pattern for prayer

To be with God wondering, that is adoration. To be with God grate-
fully, that is thanksgiving. To be with God ashamed, that is contrition.
To be with God with others on our heart, that is intercession. The secret
is the quest of God's presence; 'Thy face Lord will I seek.'

Michael Ramsey, *Be Still and Know*, pp. 73-4.

Many Christian writers have observed that if we were just able to say the Lord's Prayer once each day, and really mean it, we would not need any other prayers. Thérèse of Lisieux had this to say:

Sometimes when I'm in such a state of spiritual dryness that I can't
find a single thought in my mind which will bring me close to God, I
say an Our Father and a Hail Mary very slowly indeed.

Thérèse of Lisieux, *Autobiography of a Saint*, p. 229.

This is not as easy to do as it sounds, but it does illustrate the importance of the Lord's Prayer and the help we can gain from learning a few simple prayers off by heart. Once we have learned them they are always there and can be used at any time.

The foundation of prayer

In one of her visions Julian of Norwich heard the Lord say to her 'I am the foundation of your praying.'[1] The Lord's Prayer is the foundation of prayer, because it is given to us by Jesus who is the foundation of praying.

The Lord's Prayer shows us what prayer is all about. The Lord's Prayer sums up the faith we profess. The Lord's Prayer gives us a definition for prayer – *relationship with God for the world*.

We can also be encouraged that it is not the quantity of praying that matters, but the quality of the prayer. God is not totting up the amount of time we spend. But neither does quality refer to our eloquence. Jesus' own prayer says all we need to say. What God looks for is the eager longing of our heart. We want to spend time with God (even if we struggle miserably to get that time sorted out) and we want to be in relationship with him.

Different ways of praying

The Lord's Prayer gives us the pattern for all our praying:

1   *We come into relationship with God, we need him, we long for him* – Our Father

2   *We give God our thanks and praise* – hallowed be your name

3   *We seek God's will* – your kingdom come, your will be done. . .

4   *We bring God our needs* – give us today our daily bread

5   *We express our need of forgiveness and our desire to be forgiving* – forgive us our sins . . .

6   *We ask for strength and protection* – lead us not into temptation

These then fit into four main categories of prayer:

Adoration: the simple prayer of longing, where we pour out our heart to God; where we desire God even if we cannot find the way to express that desire. This is also the prayer of being, where we unite our will to God and seek the mind of Christ. This prayer will often be silent and it may involve meditation on God's word or contemplation of Christ as we think through what it means for us to live a Christ-like life.

Contrition: the prayer of sorrow where we humbly confess our sins and seek forgiveness and amendment of life.

Thanksgiving: joyful praise, where we lift our spirit to God in thanks for all that he has done in creation, in the redemption of the world, in the gift of the Holy Spirit, in the sustaining of the universe, and in our own lives.

Supplication: this is another word for intercession; it is when we bring our needs to God. Strictly speaking intercession is about praying for others, supplication is the whole prayer of asking. We come into the presence of

God and ask for his protection and his blessing. We are nothing without his redeeming and sustaining love.

We can also see how these four categories of prayer echo all that has been said in this part of the book: the prayer of adoration and thanksgiving is prayer with God and for God; the prayer of contrition and supplication is prayer with others and for the world.

Although this language – contrition, supplication – may seem rather dated, it is worth sticking with because it gives us an easy way to remember these four main strands of prayer. We talk about our 'Acts' of prayer, and the initial letters of the four words Adoration, Contrition, Thanksgiving, Supplication form the word Acts[2].

Now we need to act upon it.

Clothing ourselves in prayer

In what follows we will not be dealing with these different forms of prayer in any systematic way, but they are all important. They flow from Jesus' own prayer and they are the raw fibre of all Christian prayer. The specific ways of prayer we will look at will weave together these different threads in a variety of patterns, but the loom is the prayer of Christ. We should endeavour to say this prayer every day. We should try to say it with simplicity so that its truth may permeate our lives.

The Lord's Prayer ends with the word amen. This word means 'so be it'. It is a word we use at the end of every prayer. It means we agree, we give our assent. In other words, if we say a prayer we should not only mean it, we should be prepared to live it. We are making a commitment to God and to ourselves. It is for this reason that we should be careful of what we ask for in prayer. God *will* answer!

The Lord's Prayer gives us the pattern and the thread, but we need now to weave the cloth and make the garment so that we can put on a way of praying that is right for us. The words themselves are just the beginning. These words have to be enfleshed in action. We must begin to pray.

Part 2

How to pray
Opening our hands to God

Nothing so stifles prayer as our prayerful efforts.
So the first piece of practical advice is: don't try too hard.

Gerard Hughes, 'Be still and know',
The Tablet, 23 August, 1997.

1

First steps

You learn to pray by praying.

Elizabeth Obbard, *To Live is to Pray*, p. 96.

The hardest step of any journey is the first one. It is much easier to dream about the destination, to pore over guide books and maps, but sooner or later, if you are ever going to get there, you have to set off. Too many of us read about prayer (or in my case write about it) without spending enough time actually doing it.

This part of the book is designed not just to be read, but to be *used*. It is your setting off point. Hopefully, you are already getting a clearer picture of what prayer is all about: you may indeed have already started to pray, or renewed your efforts. But if you have not yet started then this part of the book provides a menu of situations where prayer can be woven into daily life and a guide to different ways of praying. The final chapter in this part is called 'Ten golden rules'. It sums up all that we will be exploring.

The first and most important step of all, is *wanting to pray*. If you have read the book this far then I think it is fair to assume that you do want to pray. You may not have started yet, and you may feel you do not want to that much, but here you are still reading, and therefore still wanting.

The second step is this: *think about the rhythms and routines of your daily life and make time for God by discerning where in each day is your time and place for prayer.*

How you answer this question will show you *how* and *when* to pray and which chapters in this part of the book will be the most helpful to you. If your life revolves around work then the chapter 'At work' might be your best next step. If you are a parent of small children then it might be the chapter 'With children'. But read through the other chapters – most of them will be relevant to everyone – and see how they shed light on how you should pray. Do not worry about skipping a chapter that does not apply to you. Use this part of the book to establish a pattern for prayer that will work through your life. Prayerfully read through the different chapters and discover those aspects of prayer that resonate with your situation.

Once you have decided what seems right just make yourself comfortable and begin.

There is not a right way, or place or posture for praying. Just the way that is right for you. Feeling comfortable is vital. You don't, for instance, have to kneel down. Sitting in an easy chair, or lying on the floor is just as good. The chapter 'With your whole being' describes some of the different ways we can use our bodies – the position we sit in, the way we hold our hands – to change the mood of our praying. All these things are important to consider.

If you are praying with someone else, agree before you start on the form the prayer is going to take. If you are planning to use set prayers, do not feel embarrassed; they are one of the best ways of getting started. Some famous prayers are printed at the end of this chapter. You can use these as the basic diet of daily prayer. It is good to learn one or two off by heart. You never know when you might be glad of a prayer you can easily recite. At the end of the book there is a list of other prayer books. If you want to use a more formal pattern of set prayers this is where to look. But do not feel your own words are not good enough. God is not interested in our eloquence but our faithfulness. And even if you have no words, offer your thoughts to God, even your distractions and your anxieties. Give him the time that you have set aside.

And do not worry if it is not very much time. It is better to set aside a few minutes in the day and stick to it, than aim for something longer and always feel guilty because you cut it short or missed it altogether. And as you begin to pray invite the Holy Spirit to pray in you, uniting your prayers to those of Jesus and to the whole company of the Church. In this way you will never be alone in your prayer.

Some primary prayers

The traditional form of the Lord's Prayer

Our Father, who art in heaven,
hallowed be thy name;
thy kingdom come;
thy will be done;
on earth as it is in heaven.
Give us this day our daily bread.
And forgive us our trespasses,
as we forgive those who trespass against us.
And lead us not into temptation;
but deliver us from evil.
For thine is the kingdom, the power and the glory,
for ever and ever. Amen.

The modern form of the Lord's Prayer as currently used in the Church of England

Our Father in heaven,
hallowed be your name,
your kingdom come,
your will be done,
on earth as in heaven.
Give us today our daily bread.
Forgive us our sins
as we forgive those who sin against us.
Lead us not into temptation
but deliver us from evil.
For the kingdom, the power and the glory are yours
now and for ever. Amen.

As we have already seen, the Lord's own prayer is the buttress of all our praying. When you are teaching the Lord's Prayer to children you need to bear in mind which version they will be saying in church and at school.

The Apostles' Creed

I believe in God, the Father Almighty,
creator of heaven and earth.
I believe in Jesus Christ, his Son, our Lord.
He was conceived by the power of the Holy Spirit
and born of the Virgin Mary.
He suffered under Pontius Pilate,
was crucified, died and was buried.
He descended to the dead.
On the third day he rose again.
He ascended into heaven,
and is seated at the right hand of the Father.
He will come again to judge the living and the dead.
I believe in the Holy Spirit,
the holy catholic church,
the communion of saints,
the forgiveness of sins
the resurrection of the body,
and the life everlasting. Amen.

We do not always think of the creed as a prayer, but it is well worth learning by heart and weaving it into daily prayer. It sums up all that we believe as Christians. Somebody said to me recently that we should recite the creed as if it were our last words as we stood before a firing squad!

The Hail Mary

Hail Mary, full of grace
the Lord is with you.
Blessed are you among women
and blessed is the fruit of your womb, Jesus.
Holy Mary, Mother of God,
pray for us sinners, now and at the hour of our death. Amen.

This prayer does not just belong to the Roman Catholic Church, as is often thought; it is a prayer for all Christians. It recalls the words of the angel to Mary as she learns of God's choosing her to be the mother of Jesus. It reminds us of our death and of our need of the prayers of others.

Prayer of St Francis of Assisi

Lord, make me an instrument of your peace:
  where there is hatred let me sow peace,
  where there is injury let me sow pardon,
  where there is doubt let me sow faith,
  where there is despair let me give hope,
  where there is darkness let me give light,
  where there is sadness let me give joy.
O Divine Master, grant that I may
  not try to be comforted but to comfort,
  not try to be understood but to understand,
  not try to be loved but to love.
Because it is in giving that we receive,
  it is in forgiving that we are forgiven,
  and it is in dying that we are born to eternal life.

This prayer speaks of the values of the kingdom of God and of how we should try to live by those values.

The Collect for Purity

> *Almighty God,*
> *to whom all hearts are open,*
> *all desires known,*
> *and from whom no secrets are hidden:*
> *cleanse the thoughts of our hearts*
> *by the inspiration of your Holy Spirit,*
> *that we may perfectly love you,*
> *and worthily magnify your holy name;*
> *through Jesus Christ our Lord. Amen.*

The Collect for Purity is the opening prayer in the Eucharist in the Anglican Church and can be found in *The Alternative Service Book* 1980. It is a wonderful prayer of preparation to receive Jesus.

The Grace

> *The grace of our Lord Jesus Christ, the love of God and the fellowship*
> *of the Holy Spirit be with us all evermore. Amen.*

This prayer reminds us that we are invited to share in the life of the Trinity. It is often used at the end of services and we can use it to end our times of prayer.

As you begin your journey of praying through life you will discover many other prayers. You may like to compile a prayer notebook of favourite prayers that seem to speak directly to your heart.

Here is a favourite of mine – a prayer for perseverance written by John Henry Newman:

> *O Lord, support us all the day long of this troublous life, until the*
> *shades lengthen, and the evening comes, and the busy world is*
> *hushed, the fever of life is over, and our work is done. Then, Lord, in*
> *your mercy grant us safe lodging, a holy rest, and peace at the last;*
> *through Jesus Christ our Lord. Amen.*

2

At home

The home is the first school of Christian life and a school for human enrichment.

Catechism of the Catholic Church.

For beginners in prayer it is very useful to build the first few attempts around the existing rhythms of life. For most Christians this will be centred in the home. This is where we spend most of our lives and this is where we are most likely to experience some rhythm in our life, even if it is only the rhythm of sleeping and waking. The home is also a place where it is most likely that we can find space where we are comfortable and available.

In the Jewish roots of Christianity the home was the liturgical centre of the faith. To this day much of the religious observance of Jewish faith takes place in the home. This was the tradition that Jesus knew, and it is striking in the gospels how often he goes to people's homes. His visits to Matthew (Matthew 9.10) and Zacchaeus (Luke 19.5-9) have a transforming effect. They also enrage his opponents. But Jesus desires to be with people where they are; he wants to make our home his home (see John 14.23).

The early Church quite naturally picked up on this tradition and much of their worship was in each other's homes. Indeed, some of the earliest Christian communities were known by the names of the owners of the homes in which they met.

There are several reasons for this. First, the early Church suffered great persecution and in many places needed to be a secret society. The much-loved fish symbol for the Christian faith originates from this time. The fish was the secret Christian sign. The first Christians worshipped in the synagogue when they could, but after the division from Judaism this was not possible. When persecution ended church buildings soon grew up.

Secondly, the early Church was a mission church. It was constantly on the move. When Jesus sent out his disciples he told them to set up base in the home of a man of peace who would welcome them (Luke 10.6). This pattern repeated itself in all the missionary endeavours of the first Christians as they took the gospel across the known world.

Thirdly, and most importantly, the early Church lived and breathed the radical belief that worship of the one true God only happens in and through Jesus. It was for proclaiming this truth that Stephen, the first Christian martyr, was stoned to death. He said that 'the Most High does not live in a house that human hands have built' (Acts 6.48). Jesus is our place of worship and our way to God, not a building or a liturgy. We need our church buildings and we need our liturgies, but they are not the essence of our faith.

In our own day we have lost the balance between worshipping in church and worshipping at home. We need to sanctify our homes. We need to let them become cells of the church, places where we are nourished, and also places of witness and service. This will happen when we restore prayer to our life at home.

Creating a place of prayer

A simple way of beginning this process is to proclaim the lordship of Jesus in your home by putting a cross on the wall, or another Christian symbol, such as a fish. This will not only remind you of your faith, it will be an unassuming witness to everyone who visits your home.

In some Christian traditions – particularly in the East, and among Afro-Caribbean Christians – great care is taken over creating a place of prayer in the home. This can be particularly helpful for children, but is something which would benefit every Christian home. It need not be elaborate. A cross, a candle, an open Bible: these things are enough to furnish a corner of a room, or an empty shelf. They provide a focus for prayer at home.

Blessing our homes

It would also be good if we could revive the tradition of prayers of blessing for our homes. This is an especially good thing to do when we move into a new home, but there is no reason why it cannot be done at any time. It could even become an annual event.

Once again this sort of service can be as simple or as complicated as you want it to be. It can involve a priest or minister visiting your home and praying with you, or it can be something you do on your own.

It can be great fun. I recently joined in some prayers of blessing on a new home and it involved us touring round the whole house swinging incense and sprinkling every room with holy water. In each room we read a verse of Scripture, and in each we prayed for God's blessing and protection. And I mean *every* room!

Here are some prayers which could be used for blessing your home:

Blessed are you, Lord God,
king of all creation:
through your goodness you have given this house to be our home.
Let your peace remain with us always.
Let all who come here to share our life
find generosity, tranquillity and happiness;
may they depart enriched by the joy of Christian living.[1]

Visit this house, O Lord, we pray,
Drive far from it all the snares of the enemy;
may your holy angels dwell with us
and guard us in peace
and may your blessing always be upon us;
through Jesus Christ our Lord. Amen.[2]

Lord Jesus Christ, who taught your apostles to bless each home they
entered with the words, 'Peace to this house': we ask your blessing on
our home. Let your peace rest upon us; keep us in your abiding love;
and be with us in our going out and in our coming in, from this time
forth and for evermore. Amen.[3]

3

Through the day

Love to pray. Feel often during the day the need for prayer, and take trouble to pray. If you want to pray better, you must pray more.

Mother Teresa of Calcutta, *In the Silence of the Heart*, p. 17.

Wouldn't it be lovely if life had the same stop, start, fast forward, rewind and pause facilities as your video recorder? Unfortunately, it is not like this except in prayer.

Prayer fast forwards us to God. The Christian life has a kind of 'already here' and 'not quite yet' feel about it. Through Jesus we already enjoy the fullness of life with God, but we are also awaiting that fullness when we shall see God face to face. It is a bit like experiencing the end of the journey in the middle. In this sense prayer is a foretaste of the banquet that awaits us in heaven. When we long for God in prayer we are united to the heart of God which longs for us.

Prayer allows us to rewind. We can be forgiven for the things that have gone wrong; we can always start again with God. We have already spoken about time not existing for God. Every single moment of human history is equidistant from God's eternity. In the Christian life everything is remembered. In prayer we can be reconciled to the past. We can be forgiven of our sins; our memories can be healed; broken relationships can be restored. We can learn to face the future because we need not be prisoners of the past. It is prayer for healing and forgiveness and reconciliation which sets us free.

Prayer allows us to stop and pause. Finding time and space to pause is the first practical foundation to put in place when we are trying to build a life of prayer. For most of us this need not be about creating *special* times, though this is clearly a good thing to do, but about building prayer into what we are *already doing*. We need to analyse the existing rhythms of our daily life and see where we can most effectively press the pause button.

Here are a few obvious places to begin:

Greeting the day

This is a lovely and fairly easy way to begin praying. As the radio alarm goes off, or as the first small child jumps onto your stomach, or as you stare at yourself in the shaving mirror, or open the curtains, or put the kettle on, or jump in the shower, or pick up the newspaper, or let out the dog, pause and pray. Most of us have some sort of getting up ritual. There are things we do nearly every day at nearly always the same time. Identify what your little routine is, and then decide when you are going to press the pause button of life and give thanks to God for another new day and for the strength you need to get through it. This prayer need only take a few seconds. You can use your own words, or you could memorise and say the same set prayer each day.

Here are some examples:

> *O Lord, enable us this day to reveal your glory in all we think and*
> *say and do; that your presence may bless and strengthen us all the*
> *day long, through Jesus Christ our Lord. Amen.*[1]

> *Lord, the smile of the dawn lights up the sky.*
> *May the smile of your face light up our day.*[2]

> *Almighty and everlasting Father,*
> *we thank you that you have brought us safely*
> *to the beginning of this day.*
> *Keep us from falling into sin*
> *or running into danger;*
> *order all our doings;*
> *and guide us to do always*
> *what is right in your eyes;*
> *through Jesus Christ our Lord. Amen.*[3]

> *Jesus, be close to me and those I love through the twists and turns of*
> *today and be with me at the day's end. Amen.*

This prayer can be said on your own, or shared with a partner. You may even discover that there is some part of your getting up routine which affords you quite a bit of time – like shaving or showering – when you can actually go through the day with God, silently offering it all to him and stilling yourself in preparation.

If, like me, you have small children, you may already be thinking that after you have been woken up that's it so far as personal time goes until the evening. In which case this may not be a way of praying that is appropriate; or it might be something which is shared with children. Indeed, changing the first nappy might be your place to pause!

Travelling

Many of us spend a lot of time each day travelling. The constant bustle and rush of modern life carries us from car to train to bus and back again. But travelling can also mean waiting – at bus stops, at stations, and most irritating of all in long queues of jammed traffic. For many of us it is travelling which shapes the rhythm of our day: journeys to work, picking up children, shopping.

If there is daily routine to the journeys you make then this is another good opportunity for prayer. In particular this might be the time for intercession. We can hardly read set prayers while driving the car, though this could be done on a train journey each day, but we could use the time in the car to pray for family and friends and for all sorts of other needs.

So much of the time spent travelling is dead time. Prayer – even if it's only for a few minutes – brings the time to life and gives the travelling another dimension of purpose. The journey to work becomes a tiny echo of the whole journey of life.

Travelling can also be very stressful and very dangerous. To pray while you are driving might be the best cure for road rage (we can replace it with motorway praise!); in our family we always begin a long journey with a moment of prayer once we are all strapped into the car.

Here is a prayer for the beginning of a journey:

> *May our Lord Jesus Christ go before us to guide us;*
> *stand behind us to give us strength;*
> *and watch over us to protect us as we travel. Amen.*

Mealtimes

Every meal is a sacred time for Christians. We are reminded that the central act of Christian worship is a meal and that the risen Christ made himself known through meals: the supper at Emmaus (Luke 24.30-31) and the breakfast on the beach (John 21.9-12). An abiding image of the Christian life is that of table fellowship with the Lord. In the book of Revelation both the acceptance of Christ as Lord, and the life of heaven itself, are described with reference to meals. 'Look I am standing at the door, knocking. If one of you hears me calling and opens the door, I will come in and share a meal at that person's side' (Revelation 3.20). 'The angel said, "Write this, Blessed are those who are invited to the wedding feast of the Lamb"' (Revelation 19.9).

Again this tradition of the sacred meal flows from our Jewish heritage. The passover meal is central to Jewish faith, and we understand our Eucharist as the Christian passover. Every week in a Jewish home through the family *seder* meal, and through the special festivals of the Jewish year which are also celebrated in the home and nearly always involve sharing food and drink, the faith is celebrated and kept alive. For Jewish children this is the chief way that they learn about their faith.

We will return to see how we can re-kindle this tradition in Christianity, but for now we need to think how we can build a moment of reflection into every meal. This is something we can each do quietly before every meal is eaten, but it is also a marvellous opportunity for shared prayer at those times when we eat together with friends and family. It has been my experience that even those friends and members of my family who are not Christians are very happy to stand around the table while the rest of us pray. It may indeed be one of the simplest and best ways of witnessing to the reality and practical relevance of faith. They too, whether they like it or not, encounter the phenomenon of God in a home and not just in a building or service.

Of course many of us very rarely eat together as a family. Shift work, fast food, hectic schedules all make it less and less likely that families sit down together to eat. We can all live together under the same roof but have very separate lives. Food is often eaten in front of the television, and as many homes have more than one set even this is not necessarily a shared experience. In one sense we need to accept a changing culture. In another we need to challenge the decline of the family meal and endeavour to ensure that as a Christian family there is at least one meal each week where we all sit down together and where there is an opportunity to pray.

When this opportunity comes the prayer should be very short. The food is for eating and I am not at all sure that God is glorified by some great long prayer that lets it go cold! This is simply a time to give thanks. The best prayers before meals are simple thanksgivings, and often set prayers are the most suitable; though, as we shall see, as children get a bit older they do like making up their own.

Here are some common examples:

> *O Lord, bless this food to our use and ourselves to your service, and keep us ever mindful of the needs of others. Amen.*

> *For what we are about to receive may the Lord make us truly thankful. Amen.*

> *In a world where so many are hungry we thank you for food.*
> *In a world where so many are lonely we thank you for each other.*
> *Amen.*[4]

And these two are slightly more elaborate. Each has a verse and response. One person says the first line and then everyone else joins in with the second.

The Lord gives food to those who fear him:
He is ever mindful of his promises. (Psalm 111.5)

The eyes of all wait upon you, O Lord:
You give them their food in due season. (Psalm 104.28)[5]

Fasting

Another way of praying is to give up the meal altogether! Fasting is a long-standing tradition of the Christian Church. Jesus would regularly abstain from food as part of his discipline of prayer, and in Matthew's gospel his teaching about fasting follows immediately from his instruction on prayer (Matthew 6.6-18).

When we fast we re-focus our lives on what is essential. We don't just deprive ourselves of luxuries – though this is also a good thing to do – but of the very things – food and drink – that our bodies consider indispensable. So indispensable, they appear to be more valuable than God. In the nakedness of the fast we acknowledge the deeper value of God. And we come back from the fast with a deeper appreciation of the gifts that God has provided which we have, for a short while, done without.

Jesus insists that we fast in secret. This is to emphasise the point that it is an encounter with God, not an outward show of religious zeal.

Fasting is a very practical way of praying. It can also be very simple. The Christian year gives us the seasons of Advent and Lent, where Christians are asked particularly to think about self-denial. Many Christians give up one meal a week as a small sign of their dependence on God.

Jesus teaches not only about prayer and fasting in this passage from Matthew's gospel, but also about almsgiving. This is no coincidence. When we fast we glimpse a little of the freedom from desire that many Christian writers have spoken of. This release gives us a new and deeper love for God, and a new respect and appreciation of the world. The most natural expression of this is giving.

This too has a practical application. If we are giving up a meal, we can at least give the money we have saved to help feed those who through no choice of their own are without food. In recent years the United Nations Children's Fund has introduced the Jar of Grace Appeal. Before each meal, or by giving up a meal each week, people are encouraged to drop a few coins into a jar and give the money to UNICEF.[6]

There are many other things that fasting can apply to other than food, especially luxuries which we come to depend on, and which sometimes appear of disproportionate value to God. We can also abstain from ways of life, habits and hobbies, and even people! It will do us no harm to go without something or somebody for a short while. Usually we will come back to the thing we have cut out with a renewed delight. One of the problems with our world today is that we have forgotten that without a fast there can be no feast. The feasting flows from the fasting. Because we have put something down, we can really appreciate picking it up again. If we try to make the whole of life a feast, we will end up enjoying nothing, or worse we might start demanding more and more because we are never satisfied. True satisfaction comes from proper appreciation. It is in abstaining that we learn this appreciation, and through it the deepest truth of all that everything comes from God. We can therefore all benefit from a discipline of fasting both to put God first, and to learn proper gratitude for the good things of the world so they neither take the place of God, nor are abused for their own sake.

In this way fasting can be like pruning. Just as individual branches have to be cut back for the whole plant to thrive, so in fasting we discover what is truly essential for life by abstaining from things which are secondary to God. If we allow ourselves to be pruned then we will be fruitful.

At the end of the day

Often we go to bed and turn over in our minds all that has happened during the day. Sometimes this can bring tremendous satisfaction; sometimes it can be ghastly. We re-live painful moments, dream up the things we should have said or should have done, plan our revenge and squirm at our failures. We all fall short of being the kind of person we want to be, let alone the person God wants us to be. When it comes to human failure and human foibles we are all past masters.

The real question is: What do we do with all this angst?

There is a Christian tradition of self-examination and confession which might properly happen at the end of the day. This can be formal, and in

Chapter 10, 'In penitence', you will find some set prayers which can be said, or it can simply help you think over the day in your head with some appropriate words of sorrow and contrition.

But at the end of the day there should also be thanksgiving. As you think over what has happened there will be cause for gratitude as well as regret. In most of our lives the grime and the glory jostle together, and by pausing for reflection you will be able to distinguish one from the other and deal with them accordingly.

Night-time can also be a time of the day when Christian couples may wish to say prayers together. This can be in bed, or in your prayer place, or anywhere in the home. Later on I will be referring to set offices of prayer which provide marvellous resources for people who feel that this is the right way of prayer for them. There is a list of appropriate books in the Further reading and resource list at the end.

The night office is called Compline, and is the shortest of them all. But here are a few simple prayers for evening and the close of the day.

> *Stay with us Lord:*
> *Behold, evening is coming,*
> *and we still have not recognised your face*
> *in each of our brothers and sisters.*
> *Stay with us, Lord Jesus Christ!*

> *Stay with us Lord:*
> *Behold, evening is coming,*
> *and we still have not shared your bread*
> *in thanksgiving with all our brothers and sisters.*
> *Stay with us, Lord Jesus Christ!*

> *Stay with us Lord:*
> *Behold, evening is coming,*
> *and we still have not recognised your Word*
> *in the words of all our brothers and sisters.*
> *Stay with us, Lord Jesus Christ!*

Stay with us Lord:
Behold, evening is coming,
and our hearts are still slow to believe
that you had to die in order to rise again.
Stay with us, Lord Jesus Christ!

Stay with us Lord:
for our night itself becomes day
when you are there!
Stay with us, Lord Jesus Christ![7]

Lighten our darkness,
Lord, we pray;
and in your mercy defend us
 from all perils and dangers of this night;
for the love of your only Son,
our Saviour Jesus Christ. Amen.[8]

Lord Jesus, the joy and beauty
of every moment of my life!

Be the last melody of my day song
as it fades into the night.

And tomorrow, when my eyes greet the morning,
be my first ray of sunlight.[9]

Save us, O Lord, while waking, and guard us while sleeping, that
awake we may watch with Christ, and when we sleep, we may rest in
peace. Amen.[10]

With children

Children who see and hear their Mums and Dads speaking with and listening to their Heavenly Father learn more about prayer than any amount of formal teaching can ever give.

Jane Keiller, *Praying with Children in the Home*, p. 5.

C hildren love to pray. Their ease with God spans Christian tradition. They are natural catholics – they thrive on routine and will be enthralled by the comfort and the colour of ritual. They are natural evangelicals – they love the word and will listen over and over again to the stories of Scripture. They are natural charismatics – their prayer will be spontaneous, joyful and creative.

As I have already mentioned, the inspiration for this book came from my experience of trying to bring up my own children in the Christian faith. Praying with them has taught me the true nature and value of prayer. It has shown me how prayer is foundational to Christian life.

When I first started to explore ways of praying together at home with small children I looked around for books on the subject. I could not find any. There are plenty of books of prayer *for* children, but nothing about how to pray *with* children. Since then I have discovered one or two, but it still seems to me that this is a terribly neglected area of Christian formation. I think back to my own parish ministry and realise I never gave any teaching, and very little encouragement, to families to pray together.

I was also interested to find out what other families did. I asked around and discovered that a great many Christian families did not pray together at all. Where there was prayer, it tended to be either children saying prayers 'privately' before they went to bed, or parents saying prayers over children as they were put to bed. Well, there is nothing wrong with any of this, but it is not the kind of praying together that we are exploring. It is not prayer through life.

If children are going to grow up knowing something of the reality of the Christian faith then they must see that reality lived out. I think many children lapse from faith because they only ever see faith as church attendance, not the day to day reality. Regular prayer together is one of the best ways to show that faith makes a difference. But we do not pray with children just to set them a good example, we pray with children because it is good in itself. We are called to be a people of prayer. Adults and children together will benefit from setting aside time for God and supporting one another in prayer. If this begins when children are small, then it can set a pattern for family life which can support the family throughout a lifetime. And even if, in later life, a child's faith begins to fade, at least they have encountered the real thing.

But as I have said, many families do not pray together, and many churches provide no teaching or encouragement, and very few books have been written about it. And as you read, you might be thinking, 'Well I've never even said a prayer with my partner, let alone with my children. And if I suggested it to my children they would probably run a mile, convinced I'd become a 'religious nutcase'. Well, the smaller the children are, the easier it is to begin. But I believe all children can and do pray. And all families, whatever the children's age, can begin praying together. So where do we begin?

Starting to pray together

With small children – say up to the age of seven – it is very important to understand something of the ways they learn and develop.

Small children need routine. The familiar boundaries of people and places and certain ways of doing things provide the conditions whereby a child can make sense of the world. Try disturbing a small child's bedtime routine and you will discover what I mean. For our children tea, television, bath, story, prayers and a good-night cuddle all need to come in the right order. For very small children you may even need to say the same things each night and make sure the right cuddly toy is in the right place in the cot before they will go to sleep. Children will do all that they can to make you conform to these rituals – and one of the best delaying tactics for bed is to extend and elaborate these routines – but in essence they are good. They echo the positive value of ritual in all areas of human life. They offer security and stability. They become the safe boundaries in which development and experiment can take place.

Small children are spontaneous. As they grow they need to be allowed to explore, to make mistakes, to go their own way. The safe boundaries of home and family are like the scaffolding around a building. If you do a good job you can take the scaffolding down.

All parents bring up their children in order to let them go. This is probably the hardest part of parenting, but it is the clearest sign of whether or not a good job has been done. Even when they are very little we need to let children express themselves in their own words and in their own way. This is good for their development; it is also a gift which adults often lose. Where we are tongue-tied and diffident, children often display a confidence and a joy.

I am always amazed at a child's ability to draw. Give a small child some paper and pencils and they will scribble with delight. Ask most adults to draw a picture and they will simmer with resentment. We seem to have been conditioned to think that we are no good at drawing. But the child does not worry about categories like 'good' or 'bad' when it comes to drawing; they just know about its joy.

Children have this amazing ability to enter deeply into the present moment. Even by the age of five, time is very vague. Everything that has gone before is yesterday. Everything which is to come is tomorrow. But what is really exciting, what really matters, is today. Children also have the ability to find great joy in little things. Buy them an expensive toy and they will play all day with the wrapping. I remember my own son tugging at my shirt when I was doing some digging in the garden, trying, vainly, to gain my attention. Eventually I stopped to see what it was he wanted. 'Daddy' he exclaimed, his eyes bright with excitement and delight. 'Worms!' He had been following behind me, and as I had turned over the clods of earth, he had been picking up big pink earthworms and collecting them in his bucket. I had seen the adult task – digging the garden; he had seen the joy of creation.

I also think of our smallest child. He has recently reached that important stage of development where he has graduated from the small plastic bath to the proper bath with his two brothers. This is a great moment, and bathtime is now a highlight of the day. When the three of them get in the bath together – the odd cross word notwithstanding – they go crazy. It is a frenzy of splashing and laughter. You need to approach the bath wearing waders and a kagoul: you know you are in the presence of serious pleasure. But when I have a bath, yes I enjoy it, it is good to rest and soak in the hot water, but, nevertheless, for me a bath is about the adult business of getting clean. For children it is the godly business of having fun.

This leads me to my final point about how children develop: children learn through play. This is the way they understand the world around them. They reproduce the world through their play, solving problems and re-enacting its dramas and delights. Play is a very serious business.

When we pray with children, especially small children, we must make sure these three elements are there. There must be ritual – the prayer must follow familiar and secure patterns. There must be spontaneity – it can't just be saying prayers, there must be opportunity for them to express their feelings and desires. There must be play – praying must be fun.

But before going on to look at how this might actually happen I want to re-emphasise the point that we can learn so much from the way children learn and the way children play. I do not want to be sentimental about children – goodness knows they can be a terrible pain when they want to – but Jesus holds before us the example of a little child as a sign of the kingdom. This is not only because we need to have trust in God, but because the child's ability to enjoy the security of his/her surroundings, to enter deeply into the joy of the present moment, and to celebrate playfully the simple fact of being, are all signs of what true Christian spirituality is about.

With children from eight to eleven, their ideas about the world are already beginning to form. They will want explanation about prayer, God, the universe and everything. Any time of prayer is likely to be interspersed with questions, and objections. But as well as wanting to find out about prayer, children will be continually offering their own insights and illuminations. In our times of prayer we must be ready to give and receive from our children. We must answer their questions as best we can and point them in the direction of a mature and meaningful understanding of the faith. We must also listen to their observations, mindful of the way God reveals his truth to little children (Matthew 11.25).

Often older children will lead the prayer. At every age we will be surprised by the way even the smallest children get to the heart of a situation by their prayer; but as children get older they need the responsibility of taking a lead. This will not just be in what is said, but in the whole way the time of prayer is managed.

What follows are ideas for developing family prayer.[1] Family does not mean Mum and Dad and 2.2 children – families today come in all shapes and sizes – it just means adults and children praying together.

Arrow prayers

We need to be alert to the countless opportunities for prayer that each day brings. Children lead exciting lives; they are always learning and discovering new things. One of the joys of parenthood is to rediscover the world through the child's eyes. When I sat down with my son and his bucket of worms I was able to re-acquaint myself with the world of worms; I was able to rediscover the joy of discovery. These moments are opportunities for prayer. This need not be forced or self-conscious. First of all, we can just make the observation, 'Isn't the world wonderful; don't we have an amazing God!' But saying a sentence of prayer – 'Thank you God for wiggly worms!' – is only a small step away.

Two guidelines seem to present themselves:

● When something new is discovered, say thank you;

● When important things are about to happen, ask for God's help and protection.

If this sort of prayer is woven into daily life, then alongside the regular pattern of prayer at bedtime and mealtimes that we shall turn to in a moment, splashes of prayer and praise will be bursting out all over the place – at the beginning of a long car journey; on the first day at a new school; setting off to cub camp; because you have just picked an especially lovely dandelion; because you have woken in the night with a bad dream; because the spellings this week are particularly hard.

Children will soon pick up on this kind of prayer. It will become second nature to offer prayers of thanks and petition throughout the day. Arising from their natural sense of wonder will be an attitude of prayerfulness that can last throughout their life.

These prayers are sometimes called 'arrow prayers'. We launch heavenward darts of longing and thanks.

Thérèse of Lisieux – often called the child of Jesus because of the wonderful simplicity of her faith – described the whole of her prayer life in a similar vein:

> For me, prayer means launching out of the heart towards God; it means lifting up one's eyes, quite simply, to heaven, a cry of grateful love, from the crest of joy or the trough of despair; it's a vast supernatural force which opens out my heart, and binds me to Jesus.

Thérèse of Lisieux, *Autobiography of a Saint*, p. 228.

As children get older these prayers can develop. While walking to school you may hear an ambulance or a fire engine. Pray for the people who are in trouble and for those rushing to help them.

There may be something in the news which troubles your child. Do not wait till bedtime prayers: an arrow prayer shared together is an instant relief. Within the madness and the emerging instability of the world, the child experiences the strong rock of faith, the constant availability of God.

Grace before meals

We have already noted how important it is for families to share meals together, and how rare it is becoming in the changed context of our daily lives. Eating is still one of the main routines that shape the day, but as children get older all sorts of other activities from television to sports clubs get in the way. One of the first things to do is make a commitment to sharing a meal together. This might only be once a week, but it is better than nothing. When the children are small it will be a lot easier, and from very early on it is possible to nurture the habit of giving thanks before we eat.

Simple prayers can soon be learned by heart and small children will appreciate the familiarity of the same prayer said each day. And simple means simple! You can start off by just saying:

> *Thank you Jesus for this food. Amen.*

From about two years old children will be able to join in, but even before this they can participate by putting their hands together and joining in the Amen.

We should not dismiss the importance of gesture and posture when children pray. Holding hands, or putting hands together in a more traditional manner, is a good way of allowing even the smallest child to participate, and help to mark out the prayer time as a special time.

Here is a traditional grace which some children will know from school:

> *For what we are about to receive may the Lord make us truly*
> *thankful. Amen.*

And another which is usually sung:

> *Thank you for the world so sweet;*
> *Thank you for the food we eat;*
> *Thank you for the birds that sing;*
> *Thank you God for everything. Amen.*[2]

As children get a bit older set prayers can give way to spontaneous prayers, or children can add their own thanksgivings to the set prayer. Some families write out their prayers on bits of card and choose a different one at each mealtime. I have even heard of a family that has made a prayer cube. Prayers are stuck on each side of the cube. The cube is then rolled at the beginning of each meal to select which prayer is said. This is certainly a good way of introducing an element of fun into the prayers.[3]

However hard it is to introduce shared prayer into family life – and I do not want to under-estimate how difficult it can be if you have never done it before – grace before meals, or before one meal, is the one thing we should all be able to do. Without allowing the food to get cold, we can thank God for each other and for his provision of our need.

Here are a few more:

> *Father, we thank you for each other, and for this food we eat. Amen.*

> *Bless this bunch as they munch their lunch.*

> *May he who blessed the loaves and fishes,*
> *Bless this family and these dishes.*

> *Praise him from whom all blessings flow;*
> *Praise him all creatures here below;*
> *Praise him above ye heavenly hosts;*
> *Praise Father, Son and Holy Ghost.*[4]

> *For coffee, tea and buttered toast,*
> *Praise Father, Son and Holy Ghost!*

Bedtime prayers

Just before bed is the best time of day for regular prayer together. You could do this in the morning, but you do not want to be swamping the day with times of prayer. The aim is to become prayerful, therefore I feel that one time of prayer each day is quite sufficient, and bedtime seems to provide the natural opportunity. Children may be more alert in the morning, but there are also a thousand other things which have to be done and hardly any time to do them. Bedtime is usually a little more relaxed.

The important thing is to let the prayer become a regular part of the bedtime routine. This routine will be different in every family, and even if both parents want to share in the prayer this will not always be possible. Nevertheless, look at your routine and see how prayer together can best be fitted in.

Here is a basic outline of what to do. But it must be adapted and developed to suit different families.[5] You needn't do exactly the same each day – though my children insist that the order remains unchanged – this is more of a menu from which you can pick the elements that might work in your situation.

Create a place for prayer

It does not need to be the same place every day, but it probably helps if it is. Children respond well to things like candles and crosses and devotional pictures. In our family we usually sit on the floor. An adult lights a candle and says, 'Jesus said . . .' and everyone replies, 'I am the light of the world.'

We place the candle next to a cross and often have other pictures according to the church season. These pictures can be talked about. As children get a bit older they can draw the pictures themselves. This can be a good Sunday thing to do – draw the picture which can be used as the icon for the prayer that week.

At special times of the year more elaborate things can be done. At Christmas a crib can be prepared, at Easter a garden. We will talk a bit more about ways of marking the church year with children in the section 'Through the year'.

Once you start thinking about the link between praying and playing you will find lots of things that can be done through the week and fed into the time of prayer.

Read a Bible story

Story-telling is often a natural part of the bedtime ritual so it fits very happily into the prayer time. You will need a good children's Bible. The Further Reading and Resource List at the end of this book gives details of some of the best ones currently available, but your local Christian bookshop should keep a good stock and sometimes it is good to browse with your children and choose one together.

Children love hearing stories, and Bible stories can be read over and over again. You can also read other Christian books during the prayer time. As children get older they can of course take turns to read themselves.

Reflect on the day

Encourage the children to think through what has happened during the day, and chip in with your own reflections – this prayer is for you as well as them. Let this lead naturally into prayers of thanksgiving and intercession. If something has happened which has been really good, say thank you. If something has happened which has been bad, say sorry. If something has happened which is worrying, seek help.

This act of reflection provides a precious opportunity for problems and concerns to be brought into the open. Prayer is a safe time when anything can be mentioned. I have found with my own children that if there is a worry at school it is usually at prayer time that it is first uncovered.

These reflections can then be gathered into a prayer by one of the adults or everybody can say a prayer in turn. By the age of three most children can frame a little thank-you prayer of their own, but I have also noticed now that my seven-year-old sometimes likes to say his prayer in his head. This is fine. We should encourage this interior life of prayer in children. It is the first sign of what we hope will be a deep and sustaining relationship of prayer in later life.

But I should also stress at this point that long and rambling prayers from adults are not suitable with children. Usually short, pithy petitions will be best; and plenty of encouragement all round, such as 'Why don't we all think of one thing that happened today that was fun', or 'Who are the people we want to pray for today?' Then everyone can just shout out their thing and not feel under pressure to make up a whole prayer.

Say the Lord's Prayer

You will be surprised how quickly children will pick up this prayer if it is said every day. Do not worry that they do not yet understand what it means. At the moment it is enough to learn the prayer off by heart and to experience it as the heart of all Christian prayer. Later on there will be time to explain its meaning.

Sing a song

It does not matter whether this is a Christian song or not. There is great joy to be found in singing, be it a nursery rhyme or a hymn. I think it is good to let the children choose what to sing. In our family, where two of the children are still very small, it is just as likely that we will sing 'Twinkle, twinkle, little star' as a Christian song. But there are lots of very good hymns for children. Some you will learn at church or school. A good resource book is *Junior Praise*, published by Marshall Pickering.

A *closing prayer*

This could be the grace or some other set prayer. It is good and helpful for small children to begin learning simple prayers off by heart. The prayers we learn in childhood we carry with us for the rest of our lives. They are always there when we need them.

There are many good books of children's prayers available. On the whole these are not very suitable for praying with children, because they are just words on a page, and do not have the vital elements of ritual, spontaneity and play which I think need to be present. But this is the point where they will be useful. Some of the best books available are in the Further Reading and Resource List at the back. Once again your local Christian bookshop will have a good selection.

Here are one or two prayers that could be used:

> *Now I lay me down to sleep*
> *I pray thee, Lord, thy child to keep;*
> *Thy love to guard me through the night*
> *And wake me in the morning light.*[6]

> *The grace of Our Lord Jesus Christ;*
> *and the love of God;*
> *and the fellowship of the Holy Spirit,*
> *be with us all evermore. Amen.*

As children get older it is worth helping them to know some of the classic prayers of the Church. These, especially, will be arrows in their quiver for later life.

> *Be thou a bright flame before me,*
> *Be thou a guiding star behind me,*
> *Be thou a smooth path below me,*
> *Be thou a kindly shepherd behind me,*
> *Today – tonight – and forever.*[7]

God be in my head,
And in my understanding;

God be in my eyes,
And in my looking;

God be in my mouth,
And in my speaking;

God be in my heart,
And in my thinking;

God be at my end,
And at my departing.[8]

After the final prayer we blow out the candle, taking it in turns each day, and then it is time for the first one to go to bed.

. I hope the ideas outlined here are fairly simple and accessible, but I am acutely aware that as many Christians never say prayers out loud outside of church services then even these ideas may seem daunting. Doubly so if it is not something you have done with your children before and you fear they will be dismissive of a sudden introduction. Begin slowly. Grace before meals and a short bedtime prayer are the least difficult starting points. Here, at least, you can rely on books and pictures to help you through your own hesitancy. But don't give up. It is easier to start when children are young, but it is possible to start at any age.

The effects of praying with your children are immense. You will restore a rhythm to daily life; you will be united in a common supplication to God; you will be providing a safe place in family life where anything can be spoken about, and an oasis where living water is always available. It has also been said that the family that prays together stays together. Undoubtedly it is true that if you pray together you and your children will experience God as the loving Father of your family and Jesus as your brother. This has to be good for family life. It need not take up a lot of time. The service I have described need only last five minutes. Its effects however are guaranteed for twenty-four hours!

5

With teenagers

*We have confused spiritual development and religious development
. . . Spiritual development is not about religion . . . it is about getting in touch with the deeper parts of life – valuing the experiences of
awe and wonder, of hurt and sorrow, relationships with other people
and the natural world and coming to an understanding of what is
meant by the term 'God'.*

Francis Cattermole, Youth A Part, p. 40.

Teenagers are interested in God. Teenagers are interested in spirituality. Teenagers may rebel against the status quo of church and
liturgy – and who could blame them? – but this does not mean they
have abandoned faith. On the contrary this is a time of life, unlike any
other, when people ask the big questions of life. I am sure that most
teenagers pray – even if they have stopped attending church; even if they
have never been to church; even if they never admit it to anyone. Each year
thousands of older teenagers and young adults flock to Taizé in France.
They go there to pray and to experience Christian community. What
teenagers need are resources to support them in their prayer, and ways of
praying together, and with others, that can support the questioning char-
acter of their spirituality.

Teenagers are inspired by the example of others. They will want to see
what the Christian faith means in action, not in theory. Books and videos
about the lives of those who have tried to live out the gospel will inspire
them to see the relevance of the Christian faith, and will tap into their own
growing hunger for justice.

The 'Further reading and resource list' at the end of the book gives a few
books that will be helpful for teenagers.

Praying with teenagers in the home

The teenage years are marked by a longing for independence. If there has been a pattern of praying together in the family there is no reason why it should not continue, but it might be the case that teenagers will want to opt out. This is normal. If family prayers do continue they will have to change to take account of the changing temperament of teenagers. If you have never prayed as a family and you have teenage children then introducing the idea of praying together will need to be done with great sensitivity. But it is not too late. Teenagers like and deserve to be treated in an adult way, and so long as they are included in all the discussion and planning there is no reason why prayer should not begin. But adults and teenagers praying together in the family is a tricky area, so please do not feel guilty if it has never happened in your family, and if you can never imagine it happening. The teenage years can be ones of huge tension between parents and children and there is no point in pretending otherwise.

But if you are planning to pray together – and once a week might be realistic – then here is a suggested outline.[1]

Silence

Light a candle or burn some incense. Teenagers respond well to atmosphere. Just have some time to be still and to think.

Recollection

This is an opportunity – either silently or aloud – to remember good things that have happened during the week and give thanks, or bad things and be sorry.

Scripture

The gospel reading set for the Sunday of that week would be a good starting point. The Youth Bible, and other Bibles, also suggest themes.

Intercession

It is important for these to be relevant to the teenager's own life and concerns, but also to reflect the needs of the world. Each person can voice a prayer in turn, or candles can be lit representing different things, or set prayers can be read out.

Here is a set intercession which could be used with older children and teenagers:

Sovereign Lord, your Son has revealed you as our heavenly Father,
from whom every family in heaven and on earth is named.
Father of all:
hear your children's prayer.

You have made your Church a spiritual family, a household of faith.
We are the brothers and sisters of Christ.
Deepen our unity and fellowship in him.
Father of all:
hear your children's prayer.

You sent your Son to give his life as a ransom for the whole human
family.
Give justice, peace and racial harmony to the world he died to save.
Father of all:
hear your children's prayer.

You gave your Son a share in the life of a family in Nazareth.
Help us to value our families, to be thankful for them,
and to live sensitively within them.
Father of all:
hear your children's prayer.

Your Son drew around him a company of friends.
Bring love and joy to all who are alone.

Help us to find in the brothers and sisters of Christ a loving family.
Father of all:
hear your children's prayer.

You are the God of the dead as well as the living.
In confidence we remember those who have gone before us.
Bring us with them to the joy of your home in heaven.
Father of all:
hear your children's prayer.[2]

Here is a general intercession, which is good for slotting in your own prayers:

Lord God, through your grace we are your people:
through your Son you have redeemed us;
in your Spirit you have made us as your own.

We pray for. . . (ourselves, our church, our home)
Make our hearts respond to your love.
Lord, receive our praise:
and hear our prayer.

We pray for. . . (our local community, our schools, our friends, things in the world)
Make our lives bear witness to your glory in the world.
Lord, receive our praise:
and hear our prayer.

We pray for. . . (people in need, Christian service)
Make our wills eager to obey, and our hands ready to heal.
Lord, receive our praise:
and hear our prayer.

We give thanks for. . .
Make our voices one with all your people in heaven and on earth.
Lord of the Church:
hear our prayer,
and make us one in heart and mind
to serve you with joy forever. Amen.[3]

Closing prayer

This again can be a set prayer.

Helping teenagers to pray together

Young people are searching for identity. With this can go self-consciousness, embarrassment, intolerance and often rebellion. Therefore, however good the relationship is between parent and teenager, and however stimulating and relevant the prayer, many young people will still not want to pray at home.

If this is the case then we need to let them know that prayer is going on and they are welcome to join in if they want to. Another idea is to encourage youth groups connected with the church to have prayer on their agenda.

While young people may be finding prayer at home impossible, and prayer in church incomprehensible, prayer together in their group with their peers might be the best way forward. Because most teenagers have a very keen spiritual awareness, what we are looking for is the right channel of expression.

Here is one way of handling prayer with teenagers that has worked in several youth groups:

Pausing

Try to create an atmosphere where it is possible to pause for a moment and be still. It needs to be as atmospheric as possible, using candles, incense, lighting, visual images, etc.

Sharing

Everyone brings something to share with everyone else. This can be a piece of personal news, a piece of music, a poem, something from the newspaper, an object – anything which means something to the person bringing it. Everyone shows what they have brought and passes it round, or if it is some music everyone listens to it, or if it is a poem or a story it is read out. If people feel comfortable they can say why they brought things.

What is brought does not have to be specifically religious. It is likely to be something like a record. To begin with there may not be anything at all. But the idea is to create a space where things of meaning and importance can be shared. As long as the leader has something to share each week, then over a period of time the young people will also start to bring things.

Reflecting

Everyone has a chance to comment on what has been brought and share what it says to them.

Praying

This leads naturally into prayer. This will not happen straight away, nor at the first few meetings, but if a time of reflection and sharing is introduced into every meeting, after a little while the young people know they have a safe place to bring things that matter to them: a place where things can be discussed and a place where they can pray for their concerns and needs. Prayer will develop slowly, and the leader needs to be sensitive both in allowing the prayer to happen and not feeling it has to be hurried. At first it will be good just to share a few things together and to sit in silence. There is nothing wrong with prayer beginning as wishful thinking and long-ing. By encouraging teenagers to sit and reflect on what matters to them, you will be leading them to prayer.

Silence

End with thoughtful quiet. Listen to some music – be guided by the young people about the right music to choose – or finish with some shared action such as lighting candles or burning incense.

The advantage of this approach to prayer with teenagers in a youth group is that everyone can participate regardless of how they feel about God or about prayer. It begins as a time of reflection and sharing, but it can become a time of intense and beautiful prayer. Sometimes very intimate things are shared. It is a great privilege to see this growing. But this is built up over time. The important first step is to establish the principle, thus demonstrating that prayer is central to the Christian faith and relevant to their lives, because it is rooted in their concerns.

Teenagers can pray. More than adults, they know that prayers are not words on a page. They will respond well to atmosphere, stillness, silence, images and symbols. They will want to live their prayer, and see prayer in action, or they will soon lose interest. Teenagers challenge the rest of us to see the connection between prayer and life. They have much to teach us.

Here are two prayers from Simon Bailey's book, *Still with God*, which capture the mood of teenage years, and show how we can learn from young people about honesty with God:

> *Today, God, I can't stop laughing.*
> *It's not that everything is funny*
> *just that everything feels happy.*
> *I keep smiling at people –*
> *and it makes them laugh as well*
> *(though some of them give me very funny looks. . .)*
>
> *Yesterday at the dentist*
> *I didn't feel like laughing –*
> *I know I can't always be happy*
> *but today I am happy and laughing*
> *so I'll keep on smiling.*
>
> *I keep bubbling over – it's your doing:*
> *you are making me happy God –*
> *you are the gladness,*
> *you're the one who keeps making me laugh,*
> *and somehow when I laugh*
> *I think I can hear you laughing as well.*
> *It's lovely.*[4]

There were wars and riots on the news tonight,
Father, and now I'm very frightened –
bombs and killings and rows don't seem too bad
in the daylight, but it's dark now. . .
I don't let other people know I'm frightened
of the dark but I am.
I'm scared of lots of things –
evil spirits and heights, being beaten up,
of pain and dying,
and even looking silly in front of my friends.
Now I'm scared of going to sleep in case I dream.

Be near me,
be a warm presence round me
and a light inside me.
You know what it's like to be very scared,
so you can help me now.
I'm nearly shivering with fright,
so help me to know you are in charge,
you know what darkness is,
you are brighter than the darkness
and warm enough to take all my shivers away.[5]

With others

Don't make your prayer life depend on the whims of the moment; make it a regular, daily practice. God is always present, always loving, and he is waiting for you.

Michel Quoist, *The Christian Response*, p. 178.

There are many different ways of praying together with other people. For most mornings of my ministry I have gathered with other priests, and sometimes lay people, to say the Office. It is not always easy to get down to the church first thing in the morning, and often I do not feel much like praying, but the presence of other people nearly always lifts my spirits and helps direct my prayer. I can also remember saying Morning Prayer on a cold April morning with a group of teenagers on a pilgrimage to Walsingham all huddled round a fire in sleeping bags. I have prayed over the telephone with people in distress. I have sat at the bedside and sung hymns with people close to death. I have said the Lord's Prayer with an old lady on the doorstep of her house after visiting her about a local issue, and ended up talking about her daughter's cancer. I have prayed with small children and marvelled at their ability to get to the heart of things. I gather with a few other Christians most Friday mornings, and we take it in turns to lead prayers and then we have breakfast together. My wife and I often sit up in bed and say Night Prayer together. I can even remember, when I was a student training for the priesthood, saying Evening Prayer out loud with five other ordinands on a crowded train going up to Durham on our way to a mission. In some respects it is quite embarrassing to recall this incident – it seems a little ostentatious – but the remarkable thing was that several other people in the carriage joined in with us. We had already been chatting a good bit to some of our fellow travellers so it was not quite the imposition it may sound. It is one of my most moving memories of shared prayer: strangers becoming pilgrims as we recited together the Lord's Prayer.

This chapter deals with two particular situations where we may pray with others – being married or single – and four particular ways of praying – in groups, using Scripture, the Daily Office and praying the psalms.

This chapter is concerned to build on the foundations of prayer we looked at in Chapters 2 and 3 in Part 2, 'At home' and 'Through the day'. That is to say we are still working on the basic premise that we need to be praying through life: prayer needs to flow from our home and be built into the daily rhythms of our ordinary life.

If you are married

It is good for partners to pray with each other. Of course there will be embarrassment if you have not done this before; of course it will take a little while to find the ways of praying that suit you best. Begin with grace before meals. Talk about your experiences as you try to build prayer into the rhythm of your daily life. Be honest with one another about what works and what doesn't. And if you are praying with children then remember this is your prayer as well. Prayer with children nourishes adults as well. But if you do not have children, or if your children have left home, or if you just want to go a bit deeper in the spiritual life, the ways of praying suggested in this section are ideal for married couples.

You may wish to begin by doing something once a week. Sunday is obviously a good day to choose, but not necessarily the best: after all you will probably have been to church. Friday or Saturday evening may be a better time, when you have a bit more space. You can think of your prayer together as preparation for Sunday.

Some couples pray together in quite a formal way every day. This is marvellous, but do not worry if it takes you a long while to get this far. As we have said already, wanting to pray *is* prayer.

Order your prayer life so that it is not a burden. Do not try to do everything at once. Be glad that you are beginning.

If you are single

Throughout this book we have spoken about how important it is for Christians to pray together in the home. Single people may have already stopped reading. I hope not. Apart from the fact that we are never alone when we pray, there are many tangible ways that single people can pray with others. There may be someone from your church whom you could meet with once a week. This person would be your prayer partner. There might be several of you in the church who would like to pray together. This is a prayer group. Some churches organise their congregations into groups of three to meet regularly for intercession. These are called prayer triplets. Single people can meet to pray in all these ways. And they need not be organised centrally in the church. It is just a matter of having the courage to seek out at least one other person who might be feeling the same way.

I am certainly aware of how difficult I find it to pray on my own. I know I am surrounded by the saints. I know there are Christian people all over the world who are praying with me. I know the Holy Spirit is praying in me. All the same I find it hard. It is a wonderful support to pray with someone else. Now I do not just *know* I am supported, I can *feel* that support.

We need also to remind ourselves that we are all single at one time or another. We presume single means unmarried, but if only one partner in a marriage is a Christian, then so far as prayer goes the other one is single. But students living away from home, people in residential care, in nursing homes, prisons, hospitals; divorced people, widowed people, those of different sexuality – all these people can be single. There are hundreds of ways of being single. All the more reason, then, to find a partner for prayer and explore some different ways of praying.

Prayer groups

Prayer groups can organise themselves in different ways. Some, like prayer triplets, meet for intercession. Here there is no particular need for set patterns, though they can be useful when beginning. Each person brings with them a number of concerns and together these are prayed for. Before missions I have known each member of the triplet pray for three people for three months. All the same, this way of praying does demand each person to feel comfortable about praying aloud without relying on books. Beginners in prayer may not feel ready for this yet. Saying your own prayers out loud takes a bit of courage at first. It is often best to begin within the framework of some set prayers. This way each person can develop at their own pace. It does not matter if someone does not speak.

The following framework is good for developing confidence in praying aloud:

Reflective Bible reading

Someone needs to lead this sort of prayer. But there is no need for the leader to have ever done it before. He or she is just the person helping everyone through. This way of praying may appear a little daunting written down here, but it is a very ancient way of praying the Scriptures and is widely used by Christians all over the world. It is particularly good for introducing people to silent reflection and praying aloud. It is good for groups where some people may have problems with reading. There is no need for anyone to look in the Bible except the person leading.

Introduction

Select a short passage of Scripture. Really any passage will do, but a story from the gospel like the call of Peter (Luke 5.1-11); or the annunciation to Mary (Luke 1.26-38); or Jesus healing the paralysed man (Mark 2.1-12); or the story of Zacchaeus (Luke 19.1-10) or the transfiguration (Mark 9.2-8) are all excellent.

Explain the whole process. In particular, before the passage is read for the first time, invite everyone to listen with their heart to see if a certain word or phrase jumps out at them. Tell them not to look at their Bibles. This is an exercise in *listening* and *waiting*. Only one person need have a Bible, though as the same passage is going to be read several times it is possible to pass the Bible round so each reading has a different voice.

The scripture is read for the first time. Everyone keeps silence together.

After this first reading keep a minute or two of silence. Which word springs out? It does not matter if it is a single word. It does not matter if the person does not know why the word strikes them or what it means. Just invite people to receive a word or phrase as if it is a gift from God.

Two minutes is a long time for people not used to silence, so be flexible as you begin. As people get used to this way of praying together so the times of silence can grow.

The scripture is read a second time. Everyone says aloud the word or phrase that struck them, if they want to.

You do not need to go round in turn. Let people speak their word or phrase into the silence. They do not need to give any explanation as to why they have selected this word. Neither do they need to make any comment as to what it might mean for them. Think rather that the word has chosen you, not you the word, and echo the word back to God. If some people choose to say nothing, that is fine. Keep another short time of silence.

The scripture is read a third time. Everyone says what they feel about their word, if they want to.

This needs to be just a sentence. People can say things like 'I feel as if God is saying . . .' or 'This makes me feel like I'm . . .' Again there is no need for explanation, just say what you feel in a simple sentence. Keep another short time of silence.

The scripture is read a fourth time. Everyone says what they feel this word means for them, if they want to.

This is also just a sentence. It is about our response to the word of God. It is about what God might be calling us to do as a result of this encounter with his word. People can say things like 'I feel as if I should . . .' or 'I think God wants me to . . .' Once again there is no need for explanation or discussion. Keep another short silence.

Everyone prays for one another.

This is where you could go round in turn, but it is probably best to just let it happen. People pray for one another, particularly praying for the things that each person has identified as their response to the word. This demands that we listen to each other as well as to God. This is the most tricky bit of the process. It might be best to begin with the person leading the group.

All this would last about twenty minutes. It is a way of praying that groups, or even couples, can regularly employ. It can be done as a personal devotion. It can be adapted in many different ways.

If you have never prayed like this it may seem strange to think of reading the same passage four times over. The actual experience of praying this way tells a different story. Often at the end people want to read the passage a fifth time! This way of looking at the Bible introduces us to the *depths* of God's word. All too often we are anxious to rush on and read the next bit. Or else we read a passage once and leave it. This method of prayer forces us to stay with a particular passage and to focus on a single word or phrase. In this way we allow the word of Scripture to be formed within us. It is a way of looking at the Scriptures where we do not read the Bible, the Bible reads us!

Even if we do not find this approach to prayer appealing, reading the Bible must be at the heart of our prayer. Bible reading notes are published by the Bible Reading Fellowship, and these are good ways into prayer, and can be shared with a partner or in a group. Other Christians prepare for church on Sunday by looking at the readings on Saturday and sharing reflections on what the Scriptures seem to be saying. Most churches follow a set pattern of readings called a Lectionary. You can either get hold of a copy of this or ask for more information from your local priest or minister.

The Daily Office

The Daily Office is the daily prayer of the Church. Stretching back to the example of the first Christian community who 'remained faithful. . . to the breaking of bread and to the prayers' (Acts 2.42), and 'regularly went to the Temple' (Acts 2.46), the main services of morning and evening prayer, and also the lesser services of mid-day prayer and night prayer, have shaped the Christian day.

Sometimes it is mistakenly thought that the Office is just for the clergy. In the Church of England, as in other churches, there is an obligation on the clergy to say the Office every day. But nowadays many lay people are not just joining the clergy in church to say morning and evening prayer, they are wanting to say the offices themselves. You can do this at home or at work, on your own or in small groups. This growth in the ordered offering of the prayer of the Church is a tremendous sign of spiritual vitality. The Church is becoming a house of prayer.

It is not possible in a book like this to give detailed outlines of the different services that make up the Office. All I can do is point you in the direction of the right books to get hold of if you want to give it a try. For Anglicans the best book available at the moment is *Celebrating Common Prayer*, a Franciscan version of the Daily Office, which can, of course, be used by Christians of all denominations. It is a most comprehensive resource book providing for services of morning, mid-day, evening and night prayer. There is what is called a simple celebration for beginners, and a smaller *Pocket Version* for travellers, or for those just wanting the main services. It is a bit tricky to understand at first, but the explanatory notes are easy to follow and your priest or minister should be able to explain it if you need some initial help.

The Roman Catholic Church has a similar book called *Morning and Evening Prayer*. This also has Night Prayer. It is taken from the Divine Office.

The Alternative Service Book and the *Book of Common Prayer*, and most prayer books of most churches, contain an Office of one sort or another. If you are thinking of trying this way of praying it would be good to seek advice from your priest and look at a few different books. Your church should be able to lend you a selection. Full details of these books, and other simple Office books such as *The Rhythm of Life: Celtic Daily Prayer* by David Adam and *Prayer in the Day* by Jim Cotter, are given in the Further Reading and Resource List at the end.

Saying an Office, even once a day, may be a bit too much for beginners. If you are going to try, then Night Prayer is the shortest and probably the easiest to fit into most daily routines. Or you could just say morning or evening prayer once a week at the weekend, or find out when the Office is said in your church and make a commitment to say it there with your clergy once a week.

The offices are also the place where 'structured and spontaneous prayer converge.'[1] This is how the notes in *Celebrating Common Prayer* describe the celebration of the Office:

> *The offering of prayer and praise to God in the form of a Daily Office is not primarily a duty to be performed but a liturgy to be celebrated in thanksgiving for the saving acts of God. We celebrate our common prayer as individuals of body, mind and spirit and as members of a community, whether large or small.*[2]

The three sections of the Office – prayers of preparation; proclamation of the Word of God; and prayers of intercession and thanksgiving – give ample room for spontaneity and silent meditation within the framework of a structured service. The prayers of preparation are usually set prayers including prayers of offering, as we place ourselves in God's presence; and penitence. The proclamation of the Word is based around the psalms and readings from Scripture. There is usually a set order for reading the psalms and during the course of a year one might read all the psalms several times over. The reading of Scripture varies a bit more. Some offices would take you right through the Bible; others have much smaller Bible passages which are intended to be read more reflectively. The prayers of intercession and thanksgiving are set prayers – collects for the day or the season and other prayers.

Praying the psalms

At the heart of the Office is the recitation of the psalms. The psalms are a bit like the prayer book of the Bible. They have always been the prayer book of the Church. Every human need and every human emotion can be found in the psalms somewhere.

Even if we are not yet ready for the whole Office, it is good for our times of shared prayer to include reading a psalm together. One of the best ways of reading the psalms is to take it in turns to read a verse. Read them slowly and quietly, allowing the words to soak into your life. But even if you are on your own it is good to say the psalms aloud. You may feel a bit of a fool at first, but persevere: it is helpful to taste the words on your tongue and hear their sound gently echo round the room. Or we can use the psalms in the same way that was described for reflective Bible reading as a whole.

The psalms are poems of lament and hymns of praise. They describe the bitter-sweet joy of pilgrimage with God. They tell of the God who is everywhere, dancing in every particle of creation. They weep at the God who seems nowhere, the hollow ache of emptiness when God seems absent. They despair at the prosperity of the wicked. They exult in God's mercy to the just. They know that it is not easy to have faith, and because of their sharp reality, they inspire us to faithfulness. We should 'read, mark, learn and inwardly digest the Scriptures', says Michael Marshall, quoting the famous Anglican Collect, 'so that they become our daily bread, feeding the imagination and the heart and getting into the subconscious which is really at the root of all our motivations'[3]. This is especially true of the psalms. They show us both the struggles and the delights of Christian life. They remind us of God's steadfast love and faithfulness. They challenge us to deeper trust in God, even in the midst of despair.

All this is summed up in the words of Psalm 13, which I quote in its entirety:

> How long, O Lord;
> will you forget me forever?
> how long will you hide your face from me?
>
> How long shall I have perplexity in my mind,
> and grief in my heart, day after day?
> how long shall my enemy triumph over me?
>
> Look upon me and answer me, O Lord my God,
> give light to my eyes, lest I sleep in death;
> Lest my enemy say, 'I have prevailed over him,'
> and my foes rejoice that I have fallen.
>
> But I put my trust in your mercy;
> my heart is joyful because of your saving help.
> I will sing to the Lord,
> for he has dealt with me richly;
> I will praise the name of the Lord Most High.

When we brood on the psalms we touch the raw nerve of discipleship.

It may take some time to develop the more structured ways of praying that we have looked at in this chapter. But our aim must be to grow in prayer and make it part of our daily life.

7

At work

The fact that I have never had any deep desire to go to Palestine and kneel at the site of the manger at Bethlehem, or rejoice at Cana where the water was turned into wine or tread the bitter road to Calvary, is simply a reflection of the fact that I have been brought up to realise that Bethlehem could be the outhouse of any pub, that all water can be made wine, and that there are Calvaries enough to spare in London and New York.

Stanley Evans, In Evening Dress to Calvary, p. 101.

Y ou can pray *anywhere* because God is *everywhere*. It is good to have places set apart for prayer – that is why we have church buildings, and that is why I have spoken about having a prayer place at home – but God is not confined to our holy places.

So far we have been concentrating on prayer in the home, in the family and with our friends. This is because it is important to see prayer as an ordinary part of life and to build prayer into the natural rhythms of life. The other natural rhythm of life for many people is work.

Praying at work

You can pray on your way to work (we have already spoken about the opportunities for prayer that we get from travelling each day). We can also pray while we work: it is good to develop a prayerful attitude to the work we do. This is a spiritual discipline that takes a little while to master. First, it is a matter of offering the work to God, to ask that God may be glorified in the work by our doing it to the best of our ability. Secondly, it is about using the work as a springboard for prayer. Many people do quite boring and repetitive work. Every job has elements of repetition within it.

Sometimes this work feels quite mindless. These little tasks can become pegs upon which we hang our prayer.

The Celtic prayer traditions are very good at showing the inter-relationship between prayer, work and all of life. This is not so obvious in the predominantly urban culture in which most of us live, but it does not mean that a similar style of spirituality cannot develop. A postman could say 'Bless this house and all who live here' as he puts each bundle of letters through the door; a long-distance lorry driver could ask God to bless each town she passes as they are sign-posted on the motorway; a packer in a canning factory could say 'Feed with your grace all who eat of this food' as each consignment is finished.

Most work connects for good with people's lives in some way or other. Look for the connections, and then in some contour of the rhythm of your work, pray for those people with whom your work connects.

Or else, simply use the repetition of the work as a peg for your own devotions. I know of people working in factories who say an 'Our Father' for each piece of work they complete. Other very simple one-sentence prayers like 'Lord have mercy', or 'Jesus is Lord' can also be said.

This way of finding God in every action and in every moment is sometimes called *the practice of the presence of God*. This comes from a beautiful little book by Brother Lawrence, a Carmelite lay brother in the eighteenth century who spent his life working in the community kitchen. He considered it a delusion to think of work time as distinct from prayer time. He found formal prayers difficult, so he tried to make each action of his life a moment of communion with God. He saw this not as a difficult accomplishment but a way of life that sprang from a simplicity of faith.

It is not always easy to pray in your work situation. Some people are exploited in their work, and some people are trapped in jobs which exploit others, or work in huge multinationals where other parts of the company's work is exploitative. Many of us are in a muddled situation. There is good in what we do, but we also know that somewhere down the line someone else is being exploited by poor wages and poor working conditions. Such is the nature of the global economy.

Here we must pray for justice. None of us is immune from the compromises and indignities of the world of work. We enjoy the rewards, we must share in the endeavour to build a fairer world. This obligation to work for justice is laid especially upon Christians. Prayer for the work we do, and witness in our place of work, are two of the principal ways that we will bring the values of God's kingdom to the day to day reality of the world.

Praying with colleagues

The place of work can also be the place we pray with others. The Church organises itself geographically. Our centres of worship are based in the centres of population: we are predominantly a neighbourhood church.

The working patterns of many people today cut across this idea. Many of us live our lives sociologically, rather than geographically. We live our lives according to the environment of our work and leisure, not the geographical environment of our house. It is not that our local neighbourhood does not have any relevance, it is just that it is more real to say we actually live at work, or in the places we go for leisure. This is our real neighbourhood insofar as this is where we build relationships and live our life: the people at work and the people we meet in our leisure are our neighbours.

For some people their actual home is not much more than a hotel room where they sleep, or a weekend retreat from their real life. We may wish it were different, but we need cells of the Church where people are actually living, not where they used to live, or where we would like them to live. Increasingly, I think this will mean that 'church', or at least expressions of church life, like small groups of Christians meeting together one lunch hour a week, or after work, will be a model for church life in the future. It will not replace the geographic, neighbourhood church, but it will be a parallel development. It may even be that in time churches will be planted into the places of work and leisure where people live most of their lives, but this is still some way off. But because work can be so all-consuming for many people, and because so many people work under such tremendous pressure, it is good to do some lateral thinking and instead of presuming prayer groups and prayer partners need to be things that happen 'after work', they can become things that are built into the rhythm of work.

It will take some courage to suggest this to colleagues, but if you do know that some of your colleagues are Christians – and if you do not, how about at least plucking up the courage to find out? – then why not raise the question with them? All the methods of prayer that have been suggested so far – reflective Bible reading, the Daily Office, the psalms, shared intercession – could be done at work with a few people forming a cell of the Church. This would be very good for the people taking part. It would be a powerful witness to other colleagues who are not Christians. I think it would also be very good for the business concerned. You might even get some sponsorship!

Wherever you happen to be

I can't face the strain of hunting in books for splendid prayers – it makes my head spin. There are such a lot of them, each more splendid than the last; how am I to recite them all, or to choose between them? I just do what children have to do before they learn to read; I tell God what I want quite simply, without any splendid turns of phrase, and somehow he always manages to understand me.

Thérèse of Lisieux, *Autobiography of a Saint*, p. 229.

We find God in the rhythm of daily life. He is the God of the familiar. We need to develop our own rituals for knowing him and getting to know him better.

These daily rituals can be said anywhere. They fit best into the rhythms of our life, but sometimes those rhythms are disturbed, and for some of us there is hardly any rhythm anyway.

I live in urban West Yorkshire. Our community is made up of a mosaic of different faiths. What is most impressive about my Muslim and Sikh neighbours is the unself-conscious way that prayer is built into daily life. There is no embarrassment about prayer, and if it is the hour of prayer then everything stops, wherever you are and whatever you are doing. I remember Richard Harris, the Bishop of Oxford, saying on *Thought for the Day* some years ago, how impressed he had been to see two Muslims praying on the forecourt of a petrol station. By contrast, many Christians will not even say grace before a meal in their own home.

If we are establishing a pattern of prayer then we must try to persevere with this prayer *wherever we are*. It is also worth learning some prayers by heart so that we can use them at any time, and in any place. The Lord's Prayer is obviously the most important, and after this it is good to choose prayers that we find helpful, or else we can learn prayers from the liturgy. It is, however, worth mentioning one particular prayer in detail.

The Jesus prayer

Just praying the name of Jesus is beautiful prayer. The name Jesus means 'God saves'. As we say his name so we invite him to be with us. 'All who call on the name of the Lord will be saved,' says Paul, echoing the words of the prophet Joel, and also Peter on the day of Pentecost (Romans 10.3; Joel 3.5; Acts 2.21).

This invocation of the name of Jesus has developed into what is known as the Jesus prayer. There are various wordings, all roughly the same. The most common is, I think,

Lord Jesus Christ, Son of the Living God, have mercy on me, a sinner.

The words combine Paul's hymn of praise to Jesus in Philippians – Jesus is the Son of God, but does not count equality with God a thing to be grasped, but empties himself to take the form of a servant (Philippians 2.6-11) – with the cry of the repentant tax collector in Luke – 'God, be merciful to me, a sinner' (Luke 8.13). As we say the prayer over and over again, breathing in on the first two phrases – 'Lord Jesus Christ, Son of the Living God' – and breathing out on the third – 'have mercy on me, a sinner', so we breathe in righteousness, and cast out sin.

It is a prayer that is meant to be said slowly, and meant to be said many times over. It is one of the simplest ways of praying. It can be said by anyone, anywhere.

This kind of prayer, where we repeat a single word or phrase, is a very good way of praying when we are feeling tired or distracted, or when we just do not know what to say to God. There are many phrases suggested by Scripture that we could learn by heart to turn to when we need prayer to be very simple.

Jesus, lead us to the Father.

Jesus, feed us with the bread of life.

Jesus, be our light in the darkness.

Jesus, send us your Spirit.

Jesus, make your home in our hearts.

Here are a few sentences suggested by Richard Foster in his book on prayer:

O Lord baptise me with love.

Jesus, let me receive your grace.

Lord Jesus, help me know that I am loved.[1]

The God of surprises

God can also be found in the disjunctures and the surprises of life. He is the God of the unexpected. He is waiting around the next corner, ready to jump out at us. Will we run and hide or will we embrace this new disclosure of his love?

It is good for us to nurture a spirit of expectation and thankfulness. 'The loving kindness of the Lord fills the whole earth', says the psalmist (Psalm 33.5). 'The world is charged with the grandeur of God,' says Gerard Manley Hopkins.[2]

I remember a few years ago watching some workmen tarmac the pavement outside my house. Just a week or so after they had finished I was amazed to see tiny shoots of green thistle emerging from the fissures, unfolding through the tar. I remember wanting to kneel down and worship. The tenacity of nature is a constant reminder of the creativity of God. Creation is not a past event but an ever present, ever moving characteristic of the creator God.

As it turned out I did not kneel down on the pavement and give thanks to God for the wonder of the world and his ever creative love; I was far too grown up. I kept on walking, even though my heart was dancing. I had not yet learned the lesson of the worms that my little son taught me.

We all need to gaze in wonder at the world and we need to be thankful. This is the prayer of adoration that is open to everyone. We need some-times just to stop and breathe in the beauty of creation and marvel at the handiwork of God. I am still re-learning this childhood skill, but it is some-thing I can heartily recommend.

With it come all sorts of other forgotten skills: I am learning again to collect conkers in the autumn, to bring home stones and driftwood from the beach, and instead of trying to snatch the odd glance as I speed along, I now stop my car and get out to marvel at the outrageous beauty of the sunsets we enjoy over the Pennines. All this is helping me to pray because it is helping me to be thankful; helping me to recover lost awe at the amazing and complex beauty of the world.

And this is not all. The way my postman is always so courteous when he delivers my letters; the cheery way the woman in the greengrocer's always slips the children a grape; the face of the old man at the bus queue setting his face against the rasping wind; the quiet dignity of the Jamaican men who removed their jackets at the graveside to fill in the grave of their father; that mother holding the shoe-box coffin of her child; all these things cause me to pray. And sometimes I want to weep for the sadness of the world; and sometimes I want to sing, because it is all so beautiful. But in it all – the grief and the glory – I am learning to see the creator God. The God who is the Father of Jesus: the God who is the Father of every human heart. The God who is known to us in Jesus, the one who leads us to prayer, because he wants to lead us to the Father.

This is how Michael Ramsey put it:

> *The praying Christian draws inspiration from the world. Sometimes the beauty he sees in the world will stir him to wonder and to worship. Sometimes the presence of the divine word in human lives of goodness or wisdom will stir him with gratitude and reverence. The presence of self-sacrifice in human lives will set him thinking of Calvary. More often perhaps the agony of the world will draw him to the compassion of Jesus and stir his will to pray.*

> Be Still and Know, p. 79.

In silence

If we really want to pray we must first learn to listen, for in the silence of the heart God speaks.

Mother Teresa of Calcutta, In the Silence of the Heart, p. 19.

All the great spiritual writers speak of the importance of silence in prayer. Jesus warns his disciples not to make a show of prayer, nor to babble to God (Matthew 6.5-6). But we live in a noisy and frantic world. We are frightened of silence. We think it will swallow us up, and we try to fill every moment with noise and activity. The radio chatters in the car; the television takes pride of place in the lounge, the chairs arranged around in homage and other sets lurk in the kitchen and the bedroom; the mobile phone is strapped to the belt; the walkman hums in the background; the computer weaves a pattern on its screen waiting to jump into life, the E-mails mounting up; the light on the fax machine flashes; the answer machine is taking a call. Our lives are busy, and just how busy tells us just how important we must be. How alien, then, it seems to switch from this feverish desire to be constantly available, constantly in touch, and be still instead.

But this is the way of prayer. God does not have a fax number; you cannot get him on the internet; he does not own a mobile phone. 'Come now and look upon the works of the Lord, what awesome things he has done on earth', says the psalmist. 'It is he who makes wars to cease in all the world, he breaks the bow and shatters the spear and burns the shield with fire. Be still, then, and know that I am God' (Psalm 46.9-11). And we might wish to add to this, 'He disconnects the computer, he silences the radio, he switches off the television set.'

Be still, and know that I am God. This stillness is not just about silence, it is about waiting on God. The awesome majesty of God should stop us in our tracks, root us to the spot, silence the frantic jabber of our minds, and bring us to our knees. This kind of silence is not emptiness, but is heavy with the mighty presence of God. The real question is this: When the Lord comes looking will he find us at home? We live so much of our life on the periphery that we often start imagining that it is the exterior things of life that really matter. What is truly important is the interior life; the life of the spirit. In the still centre of our being we need to make a home for God. Words and prayers and the Scriptures and liturgy will help us on our journey inwards, but eventually we must seek a place of silence where God can speak to us and dwell with us. 'Do you not realise', says St Paul, 'that you are a temple of God with the Spirit of God living in you?' (1 Corinthians 3.16). All this begins by finding space for God – and as we have already seen this can be anywhere – and it proceeds by clearing out within that space a place of stillness. This is not easy.

'It is hard to rear', says the poet U. A. Fanthorpe, 'rare herb of silence, through which the Word comes.'[1]

We need this silence in our prayer. It might be after we have read a passage of Scripture. It might be in the middle of an Office or some other set prayers. It might be after we have offered intercession. But wherever it occurs the silence of prayer is the centre of prayer. It is in the silence that God can speak to us. He can stir us to receive his word afresh and let his love form within us. 'Silence is the home of the Word.'[2]

If you do not find silence easy then begin with just a few moments. But as you grow in prayer, so you need also to grow in the ability to be still. Sometimes it is helpful to try taking a few deep breaths to prepare ourselves for a time of quiet. It can also be useful to use a picture or a lighted candle. Concentrating on the image before us gives us something to think about and allows us to relax and centre ourselves.

I think it is very helpful to be silent in the company of other people. There is no reason for silent prayer to be solitary prayer. The support of another person in the silence is hugely beneficial. It makes it easier to sit still and to relax into the silence. It allows us to stick with the silence when we would prefer to be busy doing something else. Silent prayer with another person or in a group creates an invisible bond. I still remember with a thankful heart different people with whom I have prayed regularly. And what I remember most is the silence we enjoyed together. In that silence we lifted one another up and helped one another to pray. I still find silence very difficult when I am on my own. I get fidgety, my mind soon starts buzzing with all sorts of other things. When I am with someone else I am able to rest in the silence. I am made more aware of the presence of Jesus, sitting at my side, enabling me to pray.

This is how Ken Leech describes silence in prayer:

> *Silence nourishes and feeds silence: the concentrated periods spill over into, and feed, the short times we manage to salvage from our day. But to create times of silent prayer and reflection each day calls for a sense of its importance and for a discipline.*

> *Spirituality and Pastoral Care*, p. 27.

I like his use of the word 'salvage'. Silence is the precious oasis of stillness that we recover from the barren desert of so much busyness. The discipline of silence, flowing from the discipline of regular prayer, and of praying with others, is not a prison that ensnares us, it is a root from which we can grow. It leads us to be prayerful and joyful in everything that we do. 'The purpose of discipline is to create the conditions of freedom.'[3]

10

In penitence

Praying is no easy matter. It demands a relationship in which you allow the other to enter into the very centre of your person, to speak there, to touch the sensitive core of your being, and allow the other to see so much that you would rather leave in darkness.

Henri Nouwen, *Seeds of Hope*, p. 66.

'If you are bringing your offering to the altar and there remember that your brother has something against you,' warns Jesus, 'leave your offering before the altar, go and be reconciled with your brother first' (Matthew 5.23-4).

Because prayer is a love affair, an exchange which draws us into ever closer relationships with God and with others, then we must be on the look out for anything which damages this relationship. Tiredness and busyness can sap the energy of prayer. But many of us are very busy leading pressured lives in an exhausting society. Often there is little we can do to spare ourselves. What we can do is limit the effect. We have already outlined simple ways that prayer can be built into the rhythm of life. This is the best way of avoiding the spiritual drought which can so often whither the Christian life. Prayer stops being another burden on an already burdened life, but becomes a part of the existing rhythm. After all Jesus does invite the overburdened to enjoy rest and assures us that his burden is light (Matthew 11.28-30). If prayer is only experienced as a chore then it is most likely that prayer has yet to find a natural place in daily living.

But the most serious obstacle to prayer is altogether more dangerous than tiredness and busyness. And it is easy to go through one's Christian life without ever properly addressing it.

The most serious obstacle to prayer is the self-centredness which unseats God from his proper place at the heart of our lives. Putting self before others is the cause of all sin. We become the centre of the universe. Other people's needs become secondary and then peripheral and then superfluous. We start imagining we are self-sufficient and very soon have placed ourselves above God.

Unrepented sin is the real barrier to prayer. It destroys relationship because it always puts self before God and before others. Pretending we are happy, we hide ourselves away from God, and if anything goes wrong we look for someone else to blame. You can see all this in the opening chapters of the Bible as we encounter not only the story of God's creative love, but also the self-centredness that spawns sin (see Genesis 3.1-13). Adam and Eve eat of the fruit that was forbidden to them. They hide themselves from God. When God confronts them about their actions Adam blames Eve, and Eve blames the serpent. They eat the fruit in the first place because they think their will is superior to God's. They hide from God by imagining they can survive without him, and also in the silent shame of their failing. They refuse responsibility for their actions and look for someone else to blame. Here is the whole human story captured in one powerful narrative. We can see the same pattern of pride and sin in our own lives. We think we know better than God. We hide from God's will. We cower in shame. We blame someone else.

The gospel of Jesus Christ is all about sin: its consequences in human lives; its defeat on the cross; and its humiliation as God offers in the risen Jesus the free gift of reconciling love to all who are penitent. Jesus both announces and embodies the possibility of reconciliation. 'Just as all die in Adam, so in Christ' (the new Adam) 'all are made alive' (1 Corinthians 15.22). Repentance – which means literally turn around – is the way we receive and live out this lasting promise of peace and forgiveness.

But even though the victory over sin is secure, this does not mean we don't carry on sinning. Obviously we do. You don't have to be a follower of Jesus Christ to see and experience the appalling consequences of human sinfulness in the world today. Injustice, oppression, exploitation, race hatred, poverty, famine and warfare are all fuelled by human greed and human pride, and all stem from the basic sin of putting self first.

As Christians we are called to be ministers of reconciliation (2 Corinthians 5.19). This means that as well as seeking forgiveness for our own failing, we must also seek justice for the world, and at the same time be ready to forgive others – even those who have seductively perpetrated the very sin we see dividing the world.

The Christian gospel is always ready to forgive. But forgiveness is not cheap. It depends upon a change of heart, putting God first, putting others before oneself. As the Lord's Prayer declares: forgive us our sins, as we forgive those who sin against us. We must be penitent – conscious of our own sin and ready to confess it to God – and generous in love to others – ready to forgive, make amends, start again. This reconciliation is much more than just saying sorry; it is about the orientation of the whole of life. Therefore we must turn around. Unless we are seeking God's forgiveness and seeking to be forgiving to others who hurt us; unless we are seeking harmony in our own relationships, then we will never be ready to go the second mile of seeking justice for the world. Our prayer will soon be very empty. We will soon find ourselves hiding away from God again.

The prophet Isaiah puts it very bluntly: 'When you stretch out your hands I turn my eyes away. You may multiply your prayers, I shall not be listening. Your hands are covered in blood' (Isaiah 1.15). But he goes on, 'Wash, make yourselves clean.'

Confessing our sins

There are three ways we can do this. First, we need to include some prayers of penitence in our daily prayer. Before bed is the best time to do this, but, of course, it does not matter when. It is good to develop a discipline of reviewing the day, giving thanks for what has been good and saying sorry for what has been damaging and hurtful. It is possible to share this with your prayer partner, but with this sort of prayer the most important person to tell is God, and do not think you have to tell anyone else. It is also good to develop this pattern of prayer with children. It is important not to be over scrupulous, nor demand that they produce a daily list of sins, but within the pattern of bedtime prayers, it is quite easy to include prayers of thankfulness and prayers of penitence. And it is wise to remember that our penitential prayers are always offered in a spirit of thanksgiving. The victory is already won; all we need do is respond to what God has already done for us in Christ. So penitential prayers need not be a miserable affair. There is joy in heaven when a sinner repents (Luke 15.7), and our hearts should be joyful that we can be forgiven.

Secondly, there are the formal prayers of penitence that we say in church. We need to prepare for these, and use them wisely to make up for the times we forget to review each day. When we arrive in church we should focus on all that God has done for us and make room in our hearts to receive him afresh by casting out the imposter sin. And we need to remember that sin is like a virus. Unless it is treated it will invade our whole being, colonise every aspect of our life, till we reach the most fatal point of all and imagine we have no need of repentance. Pride is probably the most dangerous sin of all, and if ever we find ourselves thinking we have nothing to repent, then this is when we need the grace of the gospel the most.

Thirdly, there is the actual confession of sin to God through the ministry of a priest or minister. Every church provides for this ministry in one way or another, and you can find out about this through your own church. Basically what this involves is a formal confession of sin, an opportunity to receive counsel from another person and then the assurance of forgiveness through a prayer of absolution. This is one of the most intimate and, in my view, beneficial ministries of the Church, but we have reached a point where I can only speak for myself and dare not presume to speak for any other Christian soul. All I know is that my life fails to live up to the standards of the gospel. I read the Beatitudes of Jesus and know that I am a long way from being poor in spirit, pure in heart, merciful to others and persecuted for justice. I need help in sorting out the muddle of my spiritual life. I need to receive the ministry of reconciliation so that I know that I am forgiven and so that I can model my life a little more on Christ. That is why I go to Confession once or twice a year, and I think it is something all Christians should consider. It is one sure way of keeping us humble and thankful.

Examining our conscience

Whatever way we feel is right for us to include prayers of penitence in our daily prayer, this will always begin with what is called an 'examination of conscience'. This is a slightly unwieldy phrase. All it means is looking back over our lives to see where we have done wrong; where we have fallen short of the Christian ideal; and where we have missed opportunities to do good. We compare our life to Jesus so that we can more fully orientate our life on him.

Here is a simple set of questions based around the Beatitudes, which can be used for this purpose.[1] Its emphasis is not just on what we have done wrong, but on how we can live the fullness of Christian life. It is a way of helping sort out the muddle. This is essentially a personal exercise, but it can be included in corporate prayer, either as a preparation for confession or as a source of meditation.

Blessed are the poor in spirit

Do I recognise that the world is God's – not mine? Do I express my thanks in my weekly worship? Does the world centre around me? Do I pray?

Blessed are the meek

Do I recognise that every person is created by God and equally loved by him? Does my behaviour reflect this realisation? Do I resent criticism? Do I take out my impatience on those who are weak and least likely to fight back?

Blessed are they that mourn

Do I recognise that every person is created as frail as myself and is as much in need of help and encouragement? Am I sensitive to the needs of others? Do I realise the power of my words and actions to heal or harm? Am I indifferent to the misfortune of others?

Blessed are they that hunger and thirst after justice

Do I recognise that all creation is for the good of every person and equally to be enjoyed by all? Do I steal from others the goods or the good name which belongs to them? Do I care about justice in the world? Am I lazy?

Blessed are the merciful

Do I recognise that I am myself in need of mercy? Do I ever see goodness in others? Do I make hasty judgements? Am I grateful for the forgiveness I receive from others? Am I a good steward of my time, talents and money?

Blessed are the clean of heart

Do I recognise that the heart will only rest when it is centred on God? Do I use others to try to possess them for my own satisfaction? Do I abuse the gift of sex to satisfy my own ego?

Blessed are the peacemakers

Do I recognise the source of peace, the dignity God has given me in making me one of his adopted children? Do I enjoy making trouble for others? Am I the kind of person who needs to be humoured? Am I a peacemaker?

Blessed are they that suffer persecution for the sake of justice

Do I recognise that it is in suffering that I enter most deeply into the mind of Christ? Am I prepared to stand up for what I believe? Am I prepared to make the sacrifices necessary to put my faith into action? Do I ever do penance to make up for the damage caused by my sins?

You are the salt of the earth

Do I recognise my duty to make Christ known in the world and to reveal his presence everywhere?

You are the light of the world

Do I recognise my responsibility to share the life and mission of the church? Do I hide my light away? Am I ashamed of Christ?

Do not imagine that I have come to abolish the law or the prophets. I have come not to abolish but to complete them

Do I recognise that love is the fulfilment of the law?

11

With our whole being

Prayer is not an activity of the mind, for God is not in the head. It is an activity of the whole person, and God is in the wholeness.

Ken Leech, *Soul Friend*, p. 173.

We can pray with our hands
It is very beautiful to hold a cross as we say our prayers. Sometimes just the holding can be a prayer. The feel of the cross speaks of God's sacrifice and love; words become unnecessary. Likewise we can meditate on the creation by holding a stone, or a flower or a pine-cone.

We can hold the hand of another person as we pray. This can bring enormous strength: an abstract truth – we belong to one another – becomes a felt experience. We should only do this if the other person is happy, but in group prayer, and between husband and wife, or in the family, or among those who know each other very well, holding hands as we pray expresses the relational heart of prayer in a wordless grace that lifts the spirit.

We can also lift our hands to God as we pray. This is a sign of praise.

We can hold out empty hands. This is a sign of surrender: 'nothing in my hands I bring, simply to the cross I cling'.

These are good ways of going beyond words so that our whole being is lifted to God.

There are also ancient patterns of prayer using knotted string and prayer beads. This form of prayer is very rhythmic and the passing of each knot or bead through our fingers is accompanied by a short prayer. The most famous of these forms of prayer is called the Rosary. Here a set pattern of prayers[1] is recited and for each set of prayers a different aspect of the

Christian story is brought to mind. The value of this type of prayer is its simplicity. It is easy to learn by heart and easy to follow. Once you have got into the rhythm of the prayer you can concentrate on the story of the gospel as you recite the prayers.

Prayer beads and prayer strings can also be fun for children. They will enjoy making them and enjoy using them with you. You can either follow a set pattern, like the Rosary, or make up your own patterns. Some people carry prayer beads with them in their pocket, and use them as they walk along.

We can pray with our eyes

It is good to look at the cross and ponder on the strength and depth of God's love. It is good to look at the fragile flame of a candle and ponder on our own baptismal vocation to bear the light of Christ to the world. It is good to look on the things of the world – a blade of grass or the spangled glory of a star-filled sky – and ponder on God's enterprising and expensive grace. It is good to look at icons and images of the saints and ponder on the example of their discipleship. It is good to close our eyes and let the eye of our spirit seek out the hidden beauty which is yeast to every particle of creation, raising us up to heaven and helping us see the glory in the grime of everyday life: the end in the middle.

We can pray with our ears

Music is wonderful for stilling the soul and making us ready to hear God. Music can also speak to us of mystery beyond demonstration, of truth beyond words. It does not matter if we do not know what the music means it reaches out to our spirit and touches the innermost points of our being – what we might call the gut as well as the heart. Music can make the human spirit dance.

And we should sing when we pray. This comes naturally to children, but as we get older we must work hard at being young. I think it was St Augustine who said, 'He who sings, prays twice.'

We can pray with our nose

The psalmist says, 'Let my prayer rise before you like incense' (Psalm 141.2). Smell is so evocative of place and feeling, and different things can be used in prayer to delight the senses and draw the whole of our being into our offering to God. The burning of incense reminds us of the priesthood of Jesus and of the continual offering of prayer, of which ours is just a small part; a bowl of rose petals reminds us of the heady fragrance of God and of the delights of creation.

Even breathing is an aspect of prayer. Long, deep relaxed breaths are always a good way of preparing for prayer, as is making ourselves comfortable. As we breathe out we can imagine casting out our problems; as we breathe in we can imagine receiving God's love.

We can pray with our whole body

We can prostrate ourselves in self-surrender to God; we can kneel in humility; we can sit in quiet meditation; we can hold hands in unity; we can open our palms in emptiness and in expectancy of being filled; we can stand in confidence because God's promises are sure; we can hold our hands to heaven in praise; we can roll into a ball on the floor because the pain of the world is sometimes too much to bear; we can pace in frustration as we wrestle with the will of God; we can jump and dance in sheer abandonment and joy.

Once we have realised that prayer is not just a head thing, but the response of our whole being to the love of God, then we must let the whole of our being do the praying. Our posture will reflect the mood of our prayer. We bring everything to God: and in the eternal now of his presence we can dance in delight and weep in lament.

12

Through the week

Seven whole days, not one in seven, I will praise thee.

George Herbert, 'Praise', from A *Priest to the Temple*, 1652.

The days of the week convey the different themes of the Christian story.

There is a sense in which every Thursday reminds us of Maundy Thursday. We remember Jesus' last supper with his disciples. We remember the gift of the Eucharist and how Jesus prayed for the unity of the infant Church. Thursday is a good day for praying for unity between Christians.

There is a sense in which every Friday reminds us of Good Friday. We remember the passion and death of Jesus and we pray with penitence for our own share in all that crucified him. With the penitent thief we ask to be remembered in God's kingdom. For these reasons Friday is a traditional day for fasting and abstinence.

Sunday, the first day of the week, is the day of resurrection. It is the day of new creation. It is the day when we are most likely to join with other Christians in public worship. It is church day. We remember our Baptism. We pray for new life and new vision. We seek new purpose for our own lives and for the world.

Celebrating Common Prayer also assigns different themes to the other days of the week. Monday becomes the day of the Spirit and for praying for the mission of the Church; Tuesday is concerned with waiting for the advent of Christ; Wednesday is the day of incarnation, remembering the Word made flesh; Saturday is a day of looking forward to the final consummation of all things in Christ.[1] Traditionally, Saturday is also a day when Christians remember Mary, the mother of Jesus.

Even if you do not follow all these themes it is good to observe the basic rhythm of the week by praying for unity on Thursdays, marking Friday as a penitential day, and trying always to be present at the Eucharist on Sundays.

Children will also enjoy this rhythm. Each Thursday a unity candle can be lit and prayers for other Christians can be offered. Each Friday sorry prayers can be said around a cross and a small act of abstinence shared together. Hopefully Sunday will already be a day when children are beginning to enjoy going to church, but sadly not all churches are geared up to the needs of families. An Easter candle can adorn the dinner table at home on Sundays as a way of marking the significance of the day.

As a society we no longer observe the Sabbath. This is a great loss. Every day is becoming the same. There is no longer any rhythm to the week. This puts great pressure on Christian families. Naturally there is a desire to mark Sunday, but parents do not want to have their children swimming so much against the tide of the culture that they are branded as awkward or backward. Churches are struggling to know how to respond to the secularisation of Sunday. A simple way to do this in the home is to make sure Sunday is a day where, whenever possible, everyone sits down to eat together and table prayers are said together in thanksgiving for God's new creation. The true meaning of Sabbath is not just rest from labour, but enjoyment of the creation. Trying to make Sunday a family day by worshipping, eating and re-creating together will be very close to the heart of true Sabbath.

Here is a prayer for each day of the week taken from the Simple Celebration of the Office in *Celebrating Common Prayer*:

Sunday

> *Lord of life and power,*
> *who through the mighty resurrection of your Son*
> *overcame the old order of sin and death*
> *to make all things new in him:*
> *grant that we, being dead to sin*
> *and alive to you in Jesus Christ,*
> *may reign with him in glory;*
> *to whom with you and the Holy Spirit,*
> *be praise and honour, glory and might,*
> *now and in all eternity. Amen.[2]*

Monday

Almighty God,
who sent your Holy Spirit
to be the light and life of your Church:
open our hearts to the riches of your grace
that we may bring forth the fruit of the Spirit
in love and joy and peace;
through Jesus Christ our Lord. Amen.[3]

Tuesday

O God,
who set before us the great hope
that your kingdom shall come on earth
and taught us to pray for its coming:
give us grace to discern the signs of its dawning
and to work for the perfect day
when the world shall reflect your glory;
through Jesus Christ our Lord. Amen.[4]

Wednesday

Almighty God,
who wonderfully created us in your own image
and yet more wonderfully restored us in your Son Jesus Christ:
grant that, as he came to share our human nature,
so may we be partakers of his divine glory;
who is alive and reigns with you and the Holy Spirit,
one God, now and for ever. Amen.[5]

Thursday

Almighty God,
in Christ you make all things new.
Transform the poverty of our nature
by the riches of your grace,
and in the renewal of our lives
make known your heavenly glory;
through Jesus Christ our Lord. Amen.[6]

Friday

Most merciful God,
who by the death and resurrection of your Son Jesus Christ
delivered and saved the world:
grant that by faith in him who suffered on the cross,
we may triumph in the power of his victory;
through Jesus Christ our Lord. Amen.[7]

Saturday

Merciful God,
you have prepared for those who love you
such good things as pass our understanding:
pour into our hearts such love towards you
that we, loving you above all things,
may obtain your promises,
which exceed all that we can desire;
through Jesus Christ our Lord. Amen.[8]

13

Through the year

The Church's Year has two major focal points, each proclaiming and illuminating the great acts of God in the saving events of history: the incarnation and the redemption. Each of these is centred on a double festival: the former on Christmas and Epiphany, the latter on Easter and Pentecost.

Celebrating Common Prayer, p. 680.

The Christian year enables us to enter deeply into the story of salvation. Each year we re-enact the saving work of God in the festivals of the Church.

The Christian year begins at Advent, four weeks before Christmas. It is a season of preparation for celebrating the birth of Christ and for that day when we shall meet God face to face. This longing for Christ is celebrated at Christmas itself and then meditated on through the feast of Epiphany, the manifestation of Christ to the wise men, and in the Sundays that follow. This is the cycle of the incarnation.

Lent begins on Ash Wednesday, forty days before Palm Sunday. This is the season of preparation for Easter. It is the most penitential time in the year, traditionally associated with giving things up. Holy Week, the most important week in the Christian year, begins on Palm Sunday when we remember Jesus' entrance into Jerusalem and proceeds through the great three days of Maundy Thursday, Good Friday and Holy Saturday to Easter Sunday itself, the day of resurrection. The season of Easter lasts for fifty days and reaches its climax at pentecost as we remember the gift of the Holy Spirit. This is the cycle of redemption.

The rest of the Church year is made up of lesser festivals marking the lives of the saints and the regular cycle of the year. The ones we will mention here are harvest and All Saints' tide.

There are many ways these seasons and festivals can come to life in the home and in the family. Most of those described here are going to be concerned with children, but it is important for everyone to enter into the story of faith by observing the cycles of celebration that make up the Christian year. If you use a set Office this will be catered for in the cycle of prayers and readings. If you do not then it is probably a matter of using seasonal readings from Scripture, and finding a book of prayers that marks the Christian year.

Advent

A wreath with four candles for each of the Sundays of Advent and a fifth to be lit on Christmas morning to greet the birth of Jesus is a simple and traditional way of marking Advent. The wreath can be a table decoration for Sunday dinner, or could be the focus for bedtime prayers with children. A new candle can be lit each Sunday as prayers are shared.

Advent calendars now seem to be in the shops in October along with all the other paraphernalia of Christmas. Most of them are uncompromisingly secular; but it is still possible to get Christian ones from Christian bookshops or through mail order from Christian Aid. Children will enjoy opening the windows in the build-up to Christmas. The adventurous among you may even wish to make your own Advent calendar. I have come across all sorts of variations: 24 little drawers to be opened, each containing items to create the Christmas crib; 24 pegs upon which different Christian symbols are hung; an Advent tree; 24 pockets sewn onto a large piece of cloth and again each pocket containing symbols which go to make a Christmas frieze. All of these can easily be incorporated into bedtime prayers and help children understand Advent as the countdown to Christmas, a time of getting ready to meet Jesus.

Another idea for Advent prayers with children is to re-create the journeys of Mary and Joseph, the shepherds and the wise men. Set up an empty stable and crib in one room in the house and have everyone else travelling along bookshelves from other rooms, all arriving at Christmas and Epiphany. The children will enjoy moving the figures a few inches each evening at bedtime prayers.

Christmas

Children will understand Christmas as Jesus' birthday. Making the Christmas cake a 'Happy Birthday Jesus' cake is a simple way that the Christian significance of Christmas can be re-claimed amid the inevitable excitement and activity of the day itself. In reality there is not much that can be done with small children at Christmas – they are far too excited (and parents far too exhausted) – but the small things, and going to church itself, will all help.

Children love the Christmas story. Reading the story, drawing pictures, making a crib scene are all ways of helping children enter into the drama. Making a crib is much easier than is sometimes imagined. A few cardboard toilet rolls, some old cloth, cotton wool, felt pens, glue and a little imagination (which the children will usually provide) can soon produce some Christmas figures to go in a cardboard box stable. I sometimes think it is better to improvise each year by making the crib as a family than to buy something which is simply brought out each year. But why not have both?

Lent

This starts on Ash Wednesday, but let us not forget the day before, Shrove Tuesday, Pancake day. This fun day of the year needs to be re-claimed as a Christian prelude to the season of abstinence. By all means make pancakes and have a good celebration, but also make Shrove Tuesday a day of decision – how shall we keep Lent as a family? Even the smallest children can understand the meaning of giving something up, especially if it is explained that this is about learning how much we depend on God for everything, and how the money saved is going to go to those less fortunate than ourselves.

If at all possible Lent needs to feel different without feeling miserable. Abstaining from luxuries of various kinds will make a tangible difference. But Lent can be about taking something on as well as giving something up. As children get older this can be encouraged – an extra visit to church; prayers in the morning; a regular good turn to a friend or neighbour.

In the middle of Lent comes refreshment Sunday, now invariably observed as Mothering Sunday. This has its origin in a day of rest from the fast and became associated with mothers when those in service were given leave to visit their families. Special prayers for home and family help to mark this day. Everyone can also be let off whatever they are giving up for Lent.

Holy Week and Easter

This is the week where more than any other we need to be in church to join in the great drama of salvation. But as we have already noted many churches are not ready to receive children, and often this is much worse at Easter than at Christmas. Here are some ways of celebrating at home.

Make a plain wooden cross the focus for your prayers each day. Cut out some bits of plain paper in the shape of nails. During Holy Week write sorry prayers, or single words, onto the pieces of paper and pin them on the cross. During Easter Week use colourful flower-shaped pieces of paper and write thank-you prayers, pinning each flower onto the nail, turning it into a stem.

On Maundy Thursday have some sort of Passover meal at home. Eat lamb and unleavened bread and read the story of Holy Week while you are eating.

On Good Friday eat a simple breakfast and then go without food altogether until the evening. Bake your own hot cross buns and have them when you get back from church.

During the day make an Easter garden. This is quite easy: with a little guidance small hands will quickly turn stones and twigs and moss and flowers into something quite presentable. This can either stay outside, or be constructed on a tray and brought indoors. On Easter morning the stone can be rolled away.

Easter eggs are an important part of the celebration for children. They will enjoy an Easter egg hunt, finding the eggs hidden around the house or garden. All this can easily be turned into an Easter liturgy – the Easter story can be read; prayers said around the garden and the stone rolled away; the Easter eggs sought and shared. Doing it this way helps children make the connection between the symbolism of the egg and the new life of Easter.

Pentecost

This is the birthday of the Church. We are the Church – the Spirit-filled people of God. So bake the Church a cake, sing 'Happy Birthday' and have a party at home. Children will also enjoy making things to mark pentecost; the symbols of flame and wind and water and dove easily sparking their imaginations. A pentecost mobile is a particularly good thing to make since the things that are made move in the unseen current of the air just as we have our being through the unseen movement of the Spirit. In fact, one thing that can be done at every church season is to invite children to make pictures of the stories and then to use these as icons at prayer time.

Harvest

Apart from Christmas this is the one season of the year when schools will give plenty of input. Even though most of us are cut off from the daily realities of seed-time and harvest, nothing could be more natural than giving thanks for the food we eat and praising our creator God. There is no reason why you cannot have your own harvest festival at home. This will be especially powerful if it can include flowers and other produce which the children have helped grow.

All Saints

The feast of All Saints is on 1st November. It also used to be known as 'All Hallows', and thus we have the ever more popular halloween, the eve of All Hallows, preceding it on 31st October. While much of what now happens at halloween is probably harmless fun, most Christian parents will be concerned by the pre-occupation with witches and vampires, goblins, ghosts and the devil himself that envelops our society at this time of the year, and especially our schools. I am writing this in the last week of October and just yesterday I took my children into the local newsagents after school to be greeted by a huge display of devil masks, witches' hats, toasting forks and the like. Soon there may be invitations to halloween parties and difficult decisions about whether they should go, what they should wear, not to mention concerns about what will happen at the party. Thus it is that in the past few years the Americanisation of halloween, complete with trick or treating around the streets, has come to be seen as 'normal'.

My basic position is this: I do not believe it is either necessary or normal for children to play at evil. There are dark forces at work in the world and however much fun it may be to dress up and play at all this, it is not healthy. This is not quite the same as saying it is positively harmful, and for myself I have some anxiety with Christians who get themselves into a lather over halloween but seem impervious to other evils which our society also takes for granted, such as homelessness.

What we need is a re-Christianisation of halloween. Our basic premise for this is Christ's actual victory over evil on the cross. Sin and evil are still around, but if we turn to Jesus we have a share in the victory and we have nothing to fear. Let us then hollow out our pumpkins and decorate them with Christian symbols, especially the cross, and use this as a focus for prayer at this time of the year, proclaiming Jesus as the light in the darkness. Churches should be encouraged to hold children's services at halloween. It is cathartic for us to face evil and know it to be conquered by Christ. By facing the worldly fascination with evil that lies behind the growing popularity of halloween we can restore its true association with the feast of the saints, the final sign that Christ's victory over evil is shared with all who believe in him. In this way children can still participate in halloween and even attend the parties if you are confident that it is just dressing-up, but understand it as a Christian festival.

Each year also has other festivals of the saints which capture the child's imagination and are worth celebrating in the home. March 25th, August 15th, September 8th, December 8th are all days which recall the events of the life of Mary, Jesus' mother. March 25th is nine months before Christmas: we remember the visit of the angel Gabriel. September 8th is remembered as Mary's birthday, December 8th as the date of her conception. August 15th is the day we remember Mary with Jesus in glory. Joseph is remembered on March 19th; St Francis of Assisi on October 4th. Most churches are dedicated to a saint and so the local church may have its own special day each year. The new calendar of the Church of England, called *The Christian Year: Calendar, Lectionary and Collects*, lists all these, and provides appropriate prayers, as will most church prayer books and many Christian diaries. Celebrating the saints gives us a real appreciation that we are part of a Church that is so much bigger than ourselves – a Church in heaven as well as on earth. And as we have been saying throughout this book, when we pray we are surrounded and supported by the prayers of the saints.

14

When it seems impossible

It is painful to come before God just as we are in all our poverty and nakedness; and the nearer we get to God the more we are aware of it. It's the easiest and the hardest thing to do — just to remain there with all our deficiencies and hangups, and not to pretend to be the good pious people we would like to be, but rather accepting the people we actually are.

Elizabeth Obbard, *To Live is to Pray*, pp. 46–7.

I received a Christmas card some years ago which depicted two hands clasped together against a star-filled sky. Under the picture it read: 'Faith is holding out your hand in the dark and knowing it is held'. This sounds as if it ought to be true, but is, in my opinion, a distortion of Christian spirituality. Faith is holding out your hand in the dark and *not* knowing it is held. Otherwise faith has become certainty, and this is not the Christian way. Faith is holding out your hand in the dark and *believing* it is held, even though there are times of great doubt as well as times of great faith.

The two belong together. We too often speak and act as if doubt were the opposite of faith. This is not the case. The opposite of doubt is certainty. Doubting is part of believing. This is why when people become Christians we do not ask them to say that they *know unequivocally* that God made the world, and redeemed it in Christ, but rather whether they 'believe and trust'.[1] It has to be this way since faith is relationship. People are not giving their assent to a set of abstract propositions, but to a person, the living God who is known to us as Father, Son and Holy Spirit. This is why Paul speaks of the relationship of faith between Jesus and the Church as being like a marriage (Ephesians 5.31). It is a relationship, and like all relationships will have its times of un-knowing and uncertainty, its doubts and despairs as well as its triumphs, joys and revelations.

It is often in prayer that we become most aware of the dark and difficult times of the Christian journey. There are two principal reasons why we might face a time of darkness in our faith, when we hold out our hand and it does not feel as if it is being held. The first arises from events in our lives. Something happens in our life – the death of a loved one, a serious illness, the loss of our job, the approach of our own death – that brings us face to face with issues about ourselves and about life that we had kept hidden. Sometimes this manifests itself in what feels like a loss of faith. We feel angry and resentful towards God. It feels as if God has let us down, or even abandoned us. Prayer feels impossible or suddenly feels useless. God is absent.

The second is often a work of God himself. For no particular reason prayer becomes empty, familiar words and rituals lose their comfort, church becomes boring, other Christians irritating, and faith suddenly feels a ridiculous charade. Something seems to be sapping the energy of our faith and we feel dried up.

The first thing to say is that both experiences are normal and, for most people, inevitable. Spiritual writers often speak of these experiences as being like a desert.

In Christianity the desert is a place of discovery. The people of Israel are led through the desert into the promised land. Jesus begins his ministry being driven into the wilderness. The garden of resurrection is entered through Calvary. Even though the reasons for experiencing this desert of the faith are different, often the consequences are similar. If something has happened in our life to make God feel absent, God can use that experience to nurture in us a deeper understanding of his constant presence. If we are going through a period of spiritual dryness, even if we do not know the reason, we need to begin to trust that God is leading us through this experience to a deeper understanding of his overflowing love. What troubles me is that so many Christians are ill-prepared for the dark times that will inevitably come. I feel that many people not only give up on prayer, but give up on God when they find themselves in the desert, because they were never told that this is a necessary part of faith. St John of the Cross, one of the great spiritual writers on the theme of darkness, refers to this experience as being like a dark night for the soul:

> *The Dark Night is really one continuous process of purification when we are tested to see whether we are serious in our desire for God or just interested in spiritual experiences which make us feel good about ourselves.*

Elizabeth Obbard, *To Live is to Pray*, p. 47.

By this we do not mean that God sends the difficult experiences to test us; rather he can use those experiences to help us develop in our faith. Julian of Norwich observes how the wounds of a soul that has been purified by God are seen by him as honourable scars.[2] And the tissue of a scar is stronger than the original flesh. But none of this should stop us from crying out to God when life is hard and painful. Jesus himself experienced this desolation. He pleads with God in Gethsemane that there might be another way. On the cross he experiences the absence of God and cries out: 'My God, why have you forsaken me?' (Mark 15.34).

But sometimes the periods of dryness are the work of God leading us through the desert to a maturity of faith. We need to remember that when Jesus went into the wilderness it was the Holy Spirit who was driving him there. The Spirit will drive us into the desert and we will learn utter dependency on God. So often we are tempted into thinking how good we are and how pleased God must be with us. We may even presume to look down on others. Like the potter working with the clay of a pot that is not quite right, God does not throw us away, but breaks us down and refashions us. This is a painful experience. We will feel broken and empty and feel as if we know nothing. But we need to remember that spiritual maturity is not achieved by our own hard work, but by God's grace at work in us. Often the reason God leads us into the desert is precisely because we have set too much store by our own ability. We may have started to feel that we have got faith cracked. This is the time when God will crack us. It is wise to remember that in our lives on earth the time of our most radical growth was in the darkness of unknowing during the first nine months of our lives. Here in our mother's womb, utterly dependent on someone else for every one of our needs, we grew and grew. We grew not because of our efforts or ability but because we were being fed. We were receiving not achieving. This is what can happen in the desert when we accept God's presence in the experience of his absence.

So times of darkness will come; we will find ourselves in the desert; there will be times when prayer seems impossible. When this happens we need to remember that God is with us even in the experience of his absence, and whether this is happening because of his will, or whether it is reaction to the pain of the world, God will use, and is using, these experiences to bring redemption. We have a cross-shaped faith.

In the desert we learn dependency on what really matters. Prayer will be very difficult and will often resort to simple longing, or as we have said elsewhere longing to long for God.

To help us in this time we need to be conscious of two things. First we need to remember we are on a journey – the night will give way to the dawn, the promised land does await us. Secondly, we need to look for the oasis. This will be different for every person, but if there is something that is still making sense and helping us cling on to God then we must stay with that thing whatever it is – a verse of Scripture or a familiar prayer.

The other thing that is useful on a difficult journey is a reliable guide. Well, in one sense the whole point of this experience is that we are stripped down so as to accept no guidance but that which comes from God. But in practical terms it is wise to seek the advice of a spiritual counsellor. Your priest or minister should be able to help you when you find the dark night approaching, or at the very least will be able to put you in touch with someone who can.

This darkness of faith can be the time of the most radical spiritual growth. We are pruned in order to be abundantly fruitful. We will be led to new experiences of prayer and new dependency on God. In this way we may be able to glimpse the astounding spiritual truths written of by the little known mystic St Denis:

> It is through this passing beyond yourself and every other thing (and thereby cleansing yourself from all worldly, physical, and natural love, and from everything that can be known by the normal processes of mind) that you will be caught up in love beyond the range of intellect to the super-essential ray of divine darkness. Everything else will have gone.

> St Denis, *Dionysius' Mystical Teaching*, p. 209.

As I have said throughout this book, it is unlikely that most of us will reach this intense vision of God, where even the darkness can be described as dazzling! But I include this here to reassure you that when the difficult times come it does not necessarily mean you have strayed from the path; rather it may well be that you are finding the right path at last. The Holy Spirit is leading you to new ways of praying and new ways of knowing God. You need to be prepared.

Let me finish this chapter with a beautiful prayer by Dietrich Bonhoeffer, written in prison shortly before his execution by the Nazis.

> O Lord God,
> *Great distress has come upon me;*
> *My cares threathen to crush me,*
> *and I do not know what to do.*
> *O God, be gracious to me and help me.*
> *Grant me strength to bear what you send,*
> *and do not let fear rule over me;*
> *Take a father's care of my wife and children.*
>
> *O merciful God,*
> *forgive me all the sins that I have committed,*
> *against you and against my fellow men.*
> *I trust in your grace*
> *and commit my life wholly into your hands,*
> *Do with me according to your will*
> *and as is best for me.*
> *Whether I live or die, I am with you,*
> *and you, my God, are with me.*
> *Lord, I wait for your salvation*
> *and for your kingdom.*
> *Amen.*[3]

15

Ten golden rules

Prayer is not an art to be mastered, but a way into an ever-deepening experience of the love of God through our lives.

Ralph Townsend, *Faith, Prayer and Devotion*, p. 80.

T hroughout this part of the book, as well as exploring different methods and styles of prayer, we have looked at the different situations in which we pray. This final chapter gathers together ten basic insights which give a check list and a yardstick for our developing life of prayer. Read them through carefully as a way of examining your own attitude to prayer as a result of reading this book so far and, hopefully, beginning to pray. And return to this list from time to time to keep your prayer simple and focused.

1   Start. The hardest thing about prayer is beginning. So just start. Your longing for God, and your wanting to pray, are the beginning of a relationship that can grow and grow. Tell God that you want to know him and love him, and let him make the next move.

2   Invite the Holy Spirit to pray in you and to teach you to pray.

3   Find time to pray. Set aside special times for prayer.

4   Find people to pray with, especially your family, but also friends and work mates. We need one another's support. Remember, there is no such thing as private prayer; we are surrounded by the prayers of others.

5   Build prayer into the rhythms of daily life.

6   Make your home a place of prayer.

7   Find the way of praying that is right for you. Explore different ways of praying. Listen as well as speak; give thanks as well as make

requests. Try to make sure your prayer is marked by adoration, contrition, thanksgiving and supplication, but don't let particular methods get in the way.

8   Don't look for results.

9   Make your life a prayer. Use your times of prayer to make the whole of life prayerful.

10   Don't give up when it gets hard. Trying to pray *is* praying, and God is present even in the darkness.

And as you set yourself on the way of prayer these words from the *Rule for a New Brother* may well bring you comfort:

> *Your prayer will take countless forms*
> *because it is the echo of your life,*
> *and a reflection of the inexhaustible light*
> *in which God dwells.*
>
> *Sometimes you will taste and see how good the Lord is.*
> *Be glad then, and give Him all honour,*
> *because His goodness to you has no measure.*
> *Sometimes you will be dry and joyless*
> *like parched land or an empty well.*
> *But your thirst and helplessness*
> *will be your best prayer*
> *if you accept them with patience*
> *and embrace them lovingly.*
>
> *Sometimes your prayer will be an experience*
> *of the infinite distance that separates you from God;*
> *sometimes your being and His fullness*
> *will flow into each other.*
> *Sometimes you will be able to pray*
> *only with your body and eyes;*
> *sometimes your prayer will move beyond words and images;*
> *sometimes you will be able to leave everything behind you*
> *to concentrate on God and His Word.*
> *Sometimes you will be able to do nothing else*

but take your whole life and everything in you
and bring them before God.
Every hour has its own possibilities
of genuine prayer.

So set yourself again and again
on the way of prayer.[1]

Part 3

Catching fire

My God, set me on fire

St Augustine of Hippo, *Confessions*, p.226.

1

Prayer and evangelism

When the church becomes a house of prayer the people will come running.

Brother Roger of Taizé

I recently picked up my seven-year-old son from a birthday party. He rushed to greet me brandishing a packet of glow-in-the-dark creepy crawlies that he had won in a game. We opened the packet when we got home and laid out the dozen or so green and yellow luminous insects on the kitchen table. I was fascinated to read on the back of the packet that the only energy they require is brief exposure to bright light. They will then glow in the dark for hours.

Prayer operates on the same principle. A brief exposure to the light will give us the spiritual energy to make the whole of life prayerful.

This is the vital link between prayer and evangelism that has not been spoken of enough in recent years: the single biggest reason why the Christian faith has failed to capture the hearts and minds of so many people in Britain today is that Christian people do not know how to pray. Because we do not know how to pray we are not regularly being exposed to the light of God. Because we are not regularly being exposed to the light of God we are not fulfilling the vocation of our baptism, which is to shine as lights in the world.[1] I believe the Christian faith will begin to have an impact in the life of our nation when Christian people become luminous in their faith. We need to become a church that glows in the dark.

This is how St Paul describes the process whereby we begin to shine with the reflected light of the glory of God:

> *All of us, with our unveiled faces like mirrors reflecting the glory of the Lord, are being transformed into the image that we reflect in brighter and brighter glory* (2 Corinthians 3.18).

127

And a little later on:

> It is God who said, 'Let light shine out of darkness,' that has shone
> into our hearts to enlighten them with the knowledge of God's glory,
> the glory on the face of Christ (2 Corinthians 4.6).

When Christian people begin to radiate the love of God, other people will start taking the Christian faith seriously. And although we all need regular times of prayer in order to absorb this light, in the end, as we have already noted, this inner radiance which the Scriptures speak of, is not something we achieve by hard work, or correct technique, but something we receive by grace. We rest in the presence of God, we set aside time and space for prayer, and in that exposure to the light – however brief – we are energised.

A famous story from the Desert Fathers expresses it this way:

> Abbot Lot came to Abbot Joseph and said 'Father, according as I am
> able, I keep my little rule, and my little fast, my prayers, meditation
> and contemplative silence; and according as I am able I strive to
> cleanse my heart of thoughts: now what more should I do?' The elder
> rose up in reply and stretched out his hands to heaven, and his fin-
> gers became like ten lamps of fire. He said: 'Why not be totally
> changed into fire?'[2]

We are nearing the end of a decade of evangelism. Many people thought this would be a decade of frantic activity, rushing around trying to convert as many people as possible. Actually the whole thing has been much more thoughtful. I work as the Missioner in the Anglican diocese of Wakefield and as a member of Springboard, the Archbishops of Canterbury and York initiative of the decade of evangelism, and more and more I find myself going to parishes with the intention of talking about evangelism and end-ing up talking about prayer. Many people have come to the same conclusion: that where there is no authentic spirituality there can be no effective evangelism. Robert Warren defines spirituality as 'how we encounter God and how that encounter is sustained'.[3] Therefore, if we have no encounter with God, no daily lived experience of the reality of God, then we will have nothing to show others and nothing to share with oth-ers. To put it bluntly, we cannot give what we have not got! (We cannot be luminous in our faith if we are not exposed to the light.) Our lives will be indistinguishable from other people's, save for the fact that we attend church on Sunday mornings. Our faith will appear to be nothing much more than our own chosen leisure pursuit. Prayer will make the difference. It will make the difference because it will be about putting God at the centre of life. It will make a difference because it will be a crucial first step in seeing faith as a day to day lived reality. The Christian *faith* – certain things about God and the world that we believe in – will become the Christian *life* – a whole new way of living the whole of life. And this will make life rich and joyful. Mother Teresa speaks of prayer enlarging the heart 'until it is capable of containing God's gift of himself. Ask and seek, and your heart will grow big enough to receive him and keep him as your own'.[4] And a heart which is big enough to receive God is also a heart which is small enough to let go of self, and a heart compassionate enough to show Christ's love to the world. This is the final test of effective prayer: does it make us burn with love, ache with compassion and thirst for justice? Does it open our eyes to a renewed vision for the world? Does it lift us to heaven? Does it show us the kingdom? Does it set us on fire?

2

Becoming ourselves

The blessed will not care what angle they are regarded from, having nothing to hide.

W. H. Auden, In *Praise of Limestone.*

When we pray we become ourselves as God always intended us to be. We let go of the illusion our self-image so often creates and enter into a relationship of love where our true self comes to light, knowing it is cherished and valued.

We can only truly become ourselves in this relationship. This is why prayer makes a difference. This is why Jesus Christ is hope for the whole human race.

The most striking example of this happening in the Bible is in the life of St Peter. In the gospels we find someone who is always so full of what he will do for Jesus but when it comes to the crunch he falls away.

Peter is the first of the disciples to recognise Jesus as the Christ but he cannot accept what Jesus says about the Messiah having to suffer and die. He wanted God in his own image: he wanted a conquering hero not a suffering servant. He had not yet discovered that the new life of Easter must come through the suffering of Good Friday (see Mark 8.27-31).

When Jesus appeared to a few of his disciples in his transfigured glory, Peter wanted to build some tents; he wanted to stay on the mountain keeping Jesus to himself. He had not yet discovered that the Christian faith is given in order to be given away: being a Christian will cost everything but must be given away for nothing (see Mark 9.2-8).

When Jesus walked to the disciples across the lake, Peter was the first to step out of the boat onto the water himself, but he soon started to sink. He was acting in his own strength and in his own power. He had not yet discovered that our strength is in Christ (see Matthew 14.22-33).

Jesus told a story about two houses, one built on the sand, one built on the rock. To all outward appearances the houses were identical: it was only at the time of crisis, when the storm came, that one was revealed to be useless. Without proper foundations the house on the sand collapsed (see Matthew 7.24-7).

The name Peter means rock. Jesus gave Peter this name (Matthew 16.18). In the light of all we have just said it seems a strange choice. Sandy would be a better nick-name than Rocky! In the gospels Peter is the house built on the sand. After the Last Supper, even though he had sworn that he would rather die with Jesus than disown him, Peter claims that he has not even met him (Mark 14.71).

It is then with amazement that we read about Peter in the Acts of the Apostles. Here we find someone who has been utterly transformed. Where there had been an unwillingness to see that God's grace was made strong in human weakness, there is now a bold and simple proclamation of Christ crucified and risen. 'The stone which the builders rejected is now the corner stone and in him there is salvation,' proclaims Peter (Acts 4.11).

Where there had been an unwillingness to share faith with others there is now a fearless passion to share faith with everyone. 'We cannot stop proclaiming what we have seen and heard,' says Peter (Acts 4.20).

Where there had been an unwillingness to let go of self and act in God's strength there is now humility and love. 'I have neither silver nor gold,' says Peter to a crippled beggar, 'but I will give you what I have: in the name of Jesus Christ of Nazareth, walk' (Acts 3.6).

Peter has discovered and appropriated the truth of the gospel: new life through suffering; a faith worth sharing; strength in Jesus. He has discovered this not through hard work but through God's grace.

Peter has become the rock. He has become the person he was always capable of becoming. In this sense the Christian life is always about becoming yourself. In a world which so often beguiles us into thinking we ought to be someone else this is powerful good news.

Peter has a foundation. This gives him enormous freedom. Foundations are not primarily about rooting us to the spot, but about allowing us to grow. The more weird and wonderful the building the more sure the foundation must be. In this sense the Christian life is about a new freedom to be fully human: the new life that Peter discovers does not limit his life but opens up endless new possibilities.

Peter has been exposed to the light of the risen Lord. He now radiates that light through his own life. This will have meant repentance – the casting out of those things which get in the way of our relationship with God – and prayer – making room for God that he may dwell in us. This is the fulfilment of Paul's words, 'it is no longer I, but Christ living in me' (Galatians 2.20). The Christian life is always a corporate life, a together-with-God and a together-with-one-another life. The light that shone in the face of Jesus Christ now shines in the faces of those who believe and trust in him. 'Anyone who follows me', says Jesus, 'will not be walking in the dark but will have the light of life' (John 8.12).

After the resurrection of Jesus, Peter so radiates the love of God that we are told 'the sick were taken out into the streets and laid on beds and sleeping mats in the hope that at least the shadow of Peter might fall across some of them as he went past' (Acts 5.15).

Peter is walking in the light of Christ. He reflects that light to others. Even his passing shadow brings a blessing.

This amazing story of transformation has been repeated in countless human lives throughout Christian history. We discover it in the lives of all the great saints of the Church. We discover it in our own experience. As I write this I am thinking of the holy men and women I have known who have radiated the love of God to me and who have encouraged me on my spiritual journey. Most of the people I am thinking of would probably be quite surprised if they learned how much they had influenced and inspired me. Most of them reflected the glory of God simply by the example of their lives. They did not believe themselves to be any better than anyone else – on the contrary they were acutely aware of their great need of God's forgiveness and grace – they just witnessed to the reality of God's love.

All these different people have one thing in common: they have put Jesus Christ at the centre of their life. They are people of prayer.

They will have also discovered the glorious paradox of the gospel. That if you put Jesus at the centre of your life, he will put you at the centre of his. Thus the life of prayer is a life of joy. When we glimpse the depth of God's great love for us we discover a proper love of self: a new freedom, a new confidence and an assurance that in this wonderful and dangerous universe, whatever may befall us, we are safe.

I remember sitting at the bedside of a lady who I thought was dying. Certainly she was in great pain. She had been house-bound for many years and though frustrated by her disability she gave her time to prayer, and her council flat in South London became a place of refuge and intercession where people visited to receive wise counsel and solace, and where their needs were placed before God. As we sat in silence she reached out and held my hand. 'When you feel the prick of the crown of thorns', she explained to me, 'you know he is very close.' Such was her assurance in the midst of suffering. A freedom that flowed from a life of prayer. As it turned out she made an amazing recovery, even though she was then well into her eighties. When she returned to her flat she announced that God obviously had more work for her to do. Her work was her prayer. As I write she is 100 years old, and still praying.

So this is the purpose of prayer. It is about making the whole of life an offering of praise to God. We do this by developing regular and appropriate patterns of prayer and the fruits of this will be lives that radiate the love of God. This will be good for us: we will discover new freedom and new assurance. It will be good for our families and our friends: we will discover new ways of living and a new joy in community. It will be good for the Church: we will become the praying heart that is our vocation. It will be good for the world: people will at last see the real value of the gospel.

So let us end with a vision of God. Throughout this book I have made reference to the writing of Julian of Norwich. Her thoughtful reflections on the visions she received from God have been an enormous encouragement to my faith. I think I can do no better than finish with some more of her words. This comes from the vision in which it is revealed to her that God is the foundation of our praying. I like the way she uses the word 'gaze'. This gives me great comfort when my mind wanders in prayer. We don't always need to be thinking about God; we don't always have to have something to say; we don't always need to be concentrating hard trying to listen: we can just gaze. Gazing is being, and when we gaze we can be with God in simple thanksgiving, in penitence and in wonder. He is an amazing God. Those glimpses of his grace that we catch in the fleeting moments of our prayer are the stuff of eternity. It connects our heart to the happiness we long for. 'Prayer is the means whereby we rightly understand the full-ness of joy that is coming to us.' says Julian.[1] 'There', says St Paul, 'we shall know just as fully as we are known' (1 Corinthians 13.12).

To say that human beings are made for prayer and made for relationship with God, is nothing other than saying we are made for heaven.

> We can do no more than gaze in delight with a tremendous desire to be wholly united to him, to live where he lives, to enjoy his love, and to delight in his goodness. It is then that we, through our humble, persevering prayer, and the help of his grace, come to know him now, in this present life'. This is achieved by the grace of the Holy Spirit, both now and until the time that, still longing and loving, we die. On that day we shall come to our Lord knowing our self clearly, possessing God completely'. We shall see God face to face, simply and fully. The creature, made by God, shall see and eternally gaze upon him, his Maker.

Julian of Norwich, *Revelations of Divine Love*, pp. 129–30.

When we pray we step into eternity.

A prayer

Father,
I cannot always feel you near me,
    And I know there are so many times
    I try to hide myself from you;
But still you are the searching God,
    spent in love for me,
    seeking out my heart,
    restoring and reviving.

I cannot always find the words to say,
    And you speak your word in me.
I do not always feel like praying,
    But the silent music of your song
    stirs in my indifference;
For despite my half-hearted love,
    my self-seeking desire and my pride,
    I still want you.
    And that wanting is enough;
For when I turned my back on you
    your hands received the nails.

And so I find my home in your heart:
    I am remembered in the song of the angels;
    you gather me up
    and multiply the tiny echo of my praise
    till all of heaven hears my prayer.
In you I have found my voice.

Notes

Introduction (pp. 1–9)

1. Henri Nouwen, *Seeds of Hope*, p. 73.

Part 1

1   Prayer is relationship with God (pp. 13–17)

1. Michael Marshall, *Free to Worship*, p. 3.
2. Nouwen, *Seeds of Hope*, p. 81.
3. Quoted in Anthony de Mello, *The Song of the Bird*, p. 72.

3   Prayer is relationship *for* God (pp. 22–5)

1. Michael Ramsey, *The Christian Priest Today*, p. 15.

4   Prayer is relationship with God for others (pp. 26–33)

1. Austin Farrer, *Words for Life*, p. 1.
2. Anthony de Mello, *The Song of the Bird*, p. 65.

5   A pattern for prayer (pp. 34–6)

1. Julian of Norwich, *Revelations of Divine Love*, p. 124.
2. I am not sure of the origin of this well known mnemonic. It can be found in many books on prayer. For instance, A *Manual of Catholic Devotion*, Church Literature Association, 1950, p.1.

Part 2

2   At home (pp. 45–7)

1. Adapted from A *Pocket Ritual*, p. 117.
2. *The Prayer Book as Proposed in 1928*, p. 662.
3. Adapted from Frank Colquhorn, *Comtemporary Parish Prayers*, p. 243.

3   Through the day (pp. 48–56)

1   R.H.L. Williams (ed.), *More Prayers for Today's Church*, p. 163.
2. Lucien Deiss, *Biblical Prayers*, p. 165.

3. *The Alternative Service Book* 1980, p. 60.

4. A Girl Guide world hunger grace.

5. Michael Marshall, *Free to Worship*, p. 168.

6. UNICEF can be contacted at UNICEF FREEPOST, Chelmsford, CM28BR.

7. Lucien Deiss, *Biblical Prayers*, p. 168.

8. *The Alternative Service Book* 1980, p. 70.

9. Lucien Deiss, *Biblical Prayers*, p. 180.

10. *Celebrating Common Prayer*, p. 157.

4   With children (pp. 57–68)

1. The ideas developed here were first published in the Wakefield Diocesan *Praying Away* leaflets and I am particularly grateful to Celia McCulloch who helped with material for children.

2. Mrs E. Rutter Leatham.

3. A pattern for making a 'grace cube' can be found in Ann Evans, *Room for God*, p. 91.

4. Thomas Ken (1637-1711). This is pretty much word for word the outline I wrote for *Praying Away* leaflets and is based on the prayers I say with my children each day.

5. Mary L. Duncan.

6. St Columba of Iona (*c.* 521–97).

7. Source unknown. Found in Pynson's *Horae*, 1514.

5   With teenagers (pp. 69–76)

1. This again is adapted from the Wakefield *Praying Away* leaflets.

2. Slightly adapted from *Patterns for Worship*, pp. 83–4.

3. Slightly adapted from Michael Perry (ed.), *Church Family Worship*, No. 126.

4. Simon Bailey, *Still with God*, p. 14.

5. Simon Bailey, *Still with God*, p. 36.

6   With others (pp. 77–85)

1. Michael Marshall, *Free to Worship*, p. 148. This book has a chapter on the Daily Office and is excellent for those who want to find out a bit more.

2. *Celebrating Common Prayer*, p. 684.

3   Michael Marshall, *Free to Worship*, p. 147.

8   Wherever you happen to be (pp. 90–93)

1.   Richard Foster, *Prayer*, p. 129.

2.   Gerard Manley Hopkins, 'God's Grandeur', in *Poems and Prose*, p. 26.

9   In silence (pp. 94–6)

1.   U. A. Fanthorpe, 'Friends' Meeting House, Frenchay, Bristol', No. 1 of 'Three Bristol Poems' in *Neck Verse*, p. 47.

2.   Henri Nouwen, *Seeds of Hope*, p. 10.

3.   Ken Leech, *Spirituality and Pastoral Care*, p. 28.

10   In penitence (pp. 97–102)

1.   Cottrell *et al.*, *Emmaus, the Way of Faith: Growing as a Christian*, pp. 138–9.

11   With our whole being (pp. 103–5)

1.   The Rosary is closely associated with the Roman Catholic Church and some of the prayers will not feel comfortable for some Christians of other denominations. But the Rosary is a very beautiful and meditative way of praying and well worth experimenting with. The set pattern consists of the Apostles' Creed, the Our Father, three Hail Marys, Glory be to the Father and then one Our Father, ten Hail Marys and one Glory be to the Father five times as you go round the beads. Each set of ten Hail Marys is called a decade and for each of the five decades there are five mysteries of the Christian faith to meditate on. There are three sets of Mysteries to choose from: the Joyful Mysteries: the annunciation; the visitation; the birth of Jesus; the presentation; and the finding of Jesus in the temple: secondly, the Sorrowful Mysteries: the agony in the garden; the scourging at the pillar; the crowning with thorns; carrying the cross and the crucifixion: and thirdly, the Glorious Mysteries: the resurrection; ascension; descent of the Holy Spirit; assumption of Mary; and the glory of the saints in heaven.

12   Through the week (pp. 106–9)

1.   *Celebrating Common Prayer*, p. 681.

2.   *The Alternative Service Book 1980*, p. 598.

3.   *The Alternative Service Book 1980*, p. 673.

4. *Celebrating Common Prayer*, p. 301.

5. *The Alternative Service Book* 1980, p. 450.

6. *The Alternative Service Book* 1980, p. 476.

7. *The Alternative Service Book* 1980, p. 522.

8. *The Alternative Service Book* 1980, p. 745.

14 When it seems impossible (pp. 116–20)

1. *The Alternative Service Book* 1980, Service of Baptism and Confirmation, p. 232.

2. Julian of Norwich, *Revelations of Divine Love*, p. 121.

3. Dietrich Bonhoeffer, *Letters and Papers from Prison*, pp. 170–71.

15 Ten golden rules (pp. 121–3)

1. *Rule for a New Brother*, pp. 34–5.

Part 3

1 Prayer and evangelism (pp. 127–9)

1. In the Baptism service of the Church of England the newly baptized are given a lighted candle. The priest says this is to show that they have passed from darkness to light, and the congregation replies, 'Shine as a light in the world to the glory of God the Father' (ASB, p. 233).

2. I have not been able to track down the precise origin of this well known story of the Desert Fathers, but it is certainly quoted in Thomas Merton, *The Wisdom of the Desert*, and also in the writings of Anthony de Mello.

3. Robert Warren, 'Renewing the Church around spirituality', p. 7.

4. Mother Teresa of Calcutta, *In the Silence of the Heart*, p. 17.

2 Becoming ourselves (pp. 130–34)

1. Julian of Norwich, *Revelations of Divine Love*, p. 127.

References

The Alternative Service Book 1980 (ASB).

W.H. Auden, *Collected Shorter Poems* 1927–1957, Faber, 1966.

St Augustine of Hippo, *Confessions*, trans. F. J. Sheed, Sheed and Ward, 1942.

Simon Bailey, *Still with God*, Church House Publishing, 1986.

Dietrich Bonhoeffer, *Letters and Papers from Prison*, enlarged edition, SCM Press, 1971.

The Cathechism of the Catholic Church, English translation for the United Kingdom, Geoffry Chapman/Libreria Editrice Vaticana, 1994.

Francis Cattermole, 'Audenshaw Paper no. 131', Dec. 1990 in *Youth A Part*, p. 40, Church House Publishing, 1996.

Celebrating Common Prayer, Mowbray, 1992.

Frank Colquhoun, *Contemporary Parish Prayers*, Hodder & Stoughton, 1975.

Cottrell *et al.*, *Emmaus, the Way of Faith: Growing as a Christian*, Church House Publishing, 1996.

Lucien Deiss, *Biblical Prayers*, World Library Publications, 1976.

St Denis, *Dionysius' Mystical Teaching* in *The Cloud of Unknowing and Other Works*, trans. Clifton Wolters, Penguin, 1978.

The Divine Office, Collins, 1973.

Ann Evans, *Room for God*, Church House Publishing, 1996.

Stanley Evans, *In Evening Dress to Calvary*, quoted in Ken Leech, *Spirituality and Pastoral Care*.

U. A. Fanthorpe, *Neck Verse*, Peterloo Poets, 1992.

Austin Farrer, *Words for Life*, SPCK, 1993.

Richard Foster, *Prayer*, Hodder & Stoughton, 1992.

George Guiver, *Everyday God*, Triangle, 1994.

Gerard Manley Hopkins, *Poems and Prose*, Penguin, 1953.

Julian of Norwich, *Revelations of Divine Love*, Penguin Books, 1966.

Jane Keiller, *Praying with Children in the Home*, Grove Books, 1992.

Brother Lawrence, *The Practice of the Presence of God*, Hodder & Stoughton, 1981.

Ken Leech, *Soul Friend*, Sheldon Press, 1977.

Ken Leech, *True Prayer*, Sheldon Press, 1980.

Ken Leech, *Spirituality and Pastoral Care*, Sheldon Press, 1986.

Michael Marshall, *Free to Worship*, Marshall Pickering, 1996.

Anthony de Mello, *The Song of the Bird*, Image Books, 1982.

Anthony de Mello, *The Heart of the Enlightened*, Fount, 1989.

Thomas Merton, *The Wisdom of the Desert*, Sheldon Press, 1973.

Morning and Evening Prayer, Collins, 1974.

Henri Nouwen, *Seeds of Hope*, Darton Longman and Todd, 1989.

Elizabeth Ruth Obbard, *To Live is to Pray: an Introduction to Carmelite Spirituality*, Canterbury Press, 1997.

Patterns for Worship, Church House Publishing, 1995.

Michael Perry (ed.), *Church Family Worship*, Hodder & Stoughton, 1986.

A *Pocket Ritual*, Mayhew McCrimmon, 1977.

Michel Quoist, *Prayers of Life*, Gill and Son, 1963.

Michel Quoist, *The Christian Response*, Gill and Macmillan, 1965.

Michael Ramsey, *The Christian Priest Today*, SPCK, 1972.

Michael Ramsey, *Be Still and Know*, Fount, 1982.

Rule for a New Brother, Darton, Longman and Todd, 1973.

Mother Teresa of Calcutta, *A Gift for God*, Fount, 1975.

Mother Teresa of Calcutta, *In the Silence of the Heart*, SPCK, 1983.

Thérèse of Lisieux, *Autobiography of a Saint*, trans. Ronald Knox, Fount, 1958.

Ralph Townsend, *Faith, Prayer and Devotion*, Basil Blackwell, 1983.

Robert Warren, *An Affair of the Heart*, Highland, 1994.

Robert Warren, 'Renewing the Church around spirituality', *Good News*, 26 March 1997.

Dick Williams (ed.), *More Prayers for Today's Church*, Kingsway, 1984.

Further reading and resource list

Christian bookshops usually have a vast section on spirituality and prayer. Often it is bewildering to know what to choose. If you have enjoyed this book and found it useful then here are some others which have helped me enormously. It is not supposed to be an exhaustive selection, but just a glimpse of some of the treasures, and resources, that are available. I have asterixed one book in each section which I have found particularly helpful.

Books about prayer

Richard Foster, *Prayer*, Hodder & Stoughton, 1992.

*George Guiver, *Everyday God*, Triangle, 1994.

Ken Leech, *True Prayer*, Sheldon Press, 1980.

Michael Ramsey, *Be Still and Know*, Fount, 1982.

Robert Warren, *An Affair of the Heart*, Highland, 1994.

Elizabeth Ruth Obbard, *To Live is to Pray*, Canterbury Press, 1997.

Praying Away is a pack of five short leaflets on praying as a couple without children; praying as a family with pre-school children; praying as a family with primary school children; praying as a family with teenagers; and single people praying together. It is an initiative of the Wakefield diocese in partnership with FLAME and the Mothers' Union. Copies are available from Church House, 1 South Parade, Wakefield WF1 1LP.

Books about praying with children

*Helen Albans, *Praying with Sticky Fingers*, Methodist Church Division of Education and Youth, 1992.

Steve Givens, *Building Family Prayer and Traditions*, Redemptorist Publications, 1996.

Jane Keiller, *Praying with Children in the Home*, Grove Books, 1992.

The Daily Office and other books of daily prayer

Celebrating Common Prayer, Mowbrays, 1992.

Morning and Evening Prayer, Collins, 1974.

David Adam, *The Rhythm of Life: Celtic Daily Prayer*, Triangle, 1996.

Jim Cotter, *Prayer in the Day: A Book of Mysteries*, Cairn Publications, 1987.

Books of children's prayers

*Caroline Walsh, *The Little Book of Prayers*, Kingfisher Books, 1993.

Susan Sayers, *Hello Jesus*, Kevin Mayhew, 1991.

Carol Watson, *365 Children's Prayers*, Lion, 1989.

Christian bookshops will have a wide variety of children's prayer books and Bibles. It is good to browse and find the one that seems right for you.

Children's Bibles

The Beginner's Bible, Kingsway, 1989. Very good for pre-school children.

The Lion First Bible, Lion, 1997. Very good for primary school children.

Children's Illustrated Bible, Dorling Kindersley, 1994. Excellent all round children's Bible.

Books that can be used in prayer with teenagers

*Simon Bailey, *Still with God*, Church House Publishing, 1986.

Trevor Gregory, *Serious Prayer: A Manual for Youth Leaders*, Scripture Union, 1997.

Michel Quoist, *Prayers of Life*, Gill and Son, 1963.

Youth Bible. Choose one from the selection in your local Christian bookshop.

Other books of prayers

David Adam, *Prayer Lines: Celtic Prayers about Work*, Triangle, 1992.

William Barclay, *The Plain Man's Book of Prayer*, Fount, 1959.

Michael Buckley, *A Treasury of Catholic Prayer*, Kevin Mayhew, 1979.

Frank Colquhoun, *A Little Book of Family Prayers*, Triangle, 1996.

*Lucien Deiss, *Biblical Prayers*, World Library Publications, 1976.

Christopher Herbert, *Pocket Prayers*, National Society/Church House Publishing, 1993.

Books of meditations that can be used in prayer

Anthony de Mello, *The Heart of the Enlightened*, Fount, 1989.

Anthony de Mello, *The Song of the Bird*, Image Books, 1982.

Mother Teresa of Calcutta, *A Gift for God*, Fount, 1975.

Mother Teresa of Calcutta, *In the Silence of the Heart*, SPCK, 1983.

*Henri Nouwen, *Seeds of Hope*, Darton, Longman and Todd, 1989.

Christian bookshops also stock a variety of books of meditations arranged for each day of the year.

Spiritual classics

Brother Lawrence, *The Practice of the Presence of God*, Hodder & Stoughton, 1981.

*Julian of Norwich, *Revelations of Divine Love*, Penguin Books, 1966.

Thérèse of Lisieux, *Autobiography of a Saint*, trans. Ronald Knox, Fount, 1958.

Darton, Longman and Todd also publish the 'Enfolded in Love' series of pocket books of daily readings from great spiritual writers: In *Love Enclosed*, Julian of Norwich; *By Love Alone*, Thérèse of Lisieux; *The Desert of the Heart*, The Desert Fathers; *The Heart at Rest*, St Augustine; *Lamps of Fire*, St John of the Cross; and others. The general editor of this series is Robert Llewelyn. They are an excellent introduction to the spiritual classics.

Index

The National Society
A Christian Voice in Education

The National Society (Church of England) for Promoting Religious Education supports everyone involved in Christian education – teachers, school governors, students, parents, clergy, parish and diocesan education teams – with the resources of its RE centres, courses, conferences and archives.

Founded in 1811, the Society was chiefly responsible for setting up the nationwide network of Church schools in England and Wales, and still helps them with legal and administrative advice for headteachers and governors. It was also a pioneer in teacher education through the Church colleges. The Society now provides resources for those responsible for RE and worship in any school, lecturers and students in colleges, and clergy and lay people in parish education. It publishes a wide range of books and booklets and a resource magazine, *Together with Children*.

The National Society is a voluntary body which works in partnership with the Church of England General Synod Board of Education and the Division for Education of the Church of Wales. An Anglican society, it also operates ecumenically, and helps to promote inter-faith education and dialogue through its RE centres.

For further details of the Society or a copy of our current resources catalogue and how you can support the continuing work of the Society, please contact:

The National Society
Church House
Great Smith Street
London SW1P 3NZ

Telephone: 0171-222 1672
Fax: 0171-233 2592
Email: NS@natsoc.org.uk